The
Broken

The Broken

SIOBHAN MACKENZIE

authorHOUSE®

AuthorHouse™ UK Ltd.
1663 Liberty Drive
Bloomington, IN 47403 USA
www.authorhouse.co.uk
Phone: 0800.197.4150

Published by AuthorHouse 11/09/2013

ISBN: 978-1-4918-8417-1 (sc)
ISBN: 978-1-4918-8418-8 (e)

I dedicate this book to my Grandma and Grandad.
Also to my mummy, sister, brother and daddy.
You are my rocks, my best friends, and my inspiration.
To the people who stood by me at my darkest time
I cannot thank you enough.

"If in barbed wire things can bloom, why couldn't I?
I will not die, I will not die."—
Fredl and The Children of Terezin

Please, no more.

The memories stab through the crevices of her mind. The skin, clammy, the colour of death. The quiet, so deafening, silence now taking the place of jagged breaths. The eyes, abandoned of the light that should fill them. The life that no longer dwells in these windows to the soul.

Misery, such devastating, destroying misery takes over. Poisoning any light, any happiness that could save her.

"It's okay, it's going to be okay, just relax, you will be okay I promise."

Her eyes like glass. So exhausted, but she cannot sleep. Sleep had evaded her for too long now. You can tell by the darkened skin below her eyes. Her look so lost, so full of heartache.

It's nearly the end. No hope left.

Her hair lies limp around her face. Once so blonde and full of energy. Her skin, cracked, cracking on the porcelain surface. She was once so happy, always smiling, always laughing.

Gasping. She holds on to the hand. Pleading, hoping, yearning for life to endure. Wishing desperately to wake up from this unbearable nightmare.

She is crumbling down towards the floor; declaring her pain to the emptiness around her. Nature weeps for this broken child. Her face looks back at her through the mirror. Tears stream, flooding her heart with horrific desolation.

The last breath, then nothing. Screaming. Screaming.

"Please come back. Don't leave me."

No more pain. They are in no more pain.

"Come back to me." She pleads for the light to come back to the eyes. Come back to her soul. To her family.

She stares back into the mirror. The cracks deepen down her skin; she is breaking apart, dying inside . . .

The slideshow of memories attack her being. The ones she loved. The ones she lost.

I stare into the mirror. I stare at my skin.

It is my reflection I see before me.

"I love you. Come back to me."

You may get to a point when your life will fall apart around you. It may happen slowly and gradually. Giving you time to try and prepare for the upcoming disaster. Or it may happen so suddenly, so unexpectedly, within a night your world, the whole world as far as you know it, is destroyed forever. I have had this experience, not so long ago. It has been two years since my life changed forever. I write to you to tell you my story. Our story. I hope to show you reader that if your life can fall apart around you, completely destroying who you are, that somehow, someway, you can mend yourself again. It may feel like your whole life has shattered into little glass pieces. They lie on the floor near you. And it is you and only you, who can find a way to pick them all up and put them back together again. Hopefully not cutting yourself too deeply in the process. Maybe when you manage to put life back together you put it back another way. Not in the form you first intended, but a form you can be happy with none the less.

I intend to put mine back another way. I would be lying if I said I was not terrified, because I am. The shards of glass around me make up my life, and there are only a couple of pieces I can manage to gather. They are travel and writing. So I intend to do both. I have nothing to give anyone; I have nothing to give myself. I have only a desire to be happy. I can only hope I have the strength to make that happen.

Part One

1

The Florida sun was intense. Burning down with brutal vengeance, tracking your every move. We had hoped to find relief in the rented car we were given. We were seriously mistaken. The sun's heat had seeped through the window screen, causing the interior to become somewhat of a human oven. Being British the complaints started immediately, but I hope you can see our reasons behind it. However being typical us, the complaints did not last long, and we were soon laughing.

The rest of the drive passed in a blur, but at some point in this journey a NASA space shuttle took off from its base. I can still imagine the beautiful pointed rocket thrown into the sky carrying lucky men and women inside, about to bask in the glory of space. Unfortunately I can only imagine as I don't remember it. How can my brain forget something as extraordinary as that? Maybe one day I can be there to witness another one. Maybe.

My next memory was a glorious one. We were at Disneyland! Seeing the castle for the first time truly felt like a fairy tale. How Cinderella must have felt when she arrived at the ball, seeing this magical place, full of wonder and dreams and magic!

My dad showed me which of the rooms the princesses slept in. With Mickey Mouse being in the top tower of the castle. I could almost see it, the princesses putting on their dresses, and Minnie with her bow. How beautifully naive.

I remember eating a chocolate cake the size of my head and devouring it all! Enjoying a boat ride through a tunnel lined with singing dolls. Walking into a shop that sold a variety of Mexican hats, which I desperately wanted but could not get.

But the one day I hold so close to my heart, with so much happiness and hope, the most beautiful day I remember with clarity as clear as crystal, was the day of the parade. We stood in a crowd of thousands. Waiting in anticipation for what? Waiting for something, anything! Wondering what magic we would see, what wonderful worlds we were about to experience. All of a sudden the crowd went silent. We knew something was about to happen, the speakers came on and a song filled the air, 'When you wish upon a star,' if you're a real Disney fan you should know this song from the film 'Pinocchio'. The crowd lit up, a slow buzz of excitement was heard from the beginning of the crowd. Something was coming, but what! The song continued and as I was beginning to give up hope, I finally saw it. The first float, Cinderella was waving at us all; next to her was her prince. Then Ariel sat so elegantly in a large pearl shell. Belle, in her beautiful ball gown, and the Beast dancing. Circling them was a tea pot, a clock and candle sticks! Other beautiful scenes followed. Aladdin and Jasmine on a magic carpet, Mufasa and Simba on top of Pride Rock! Snow White, Peter Pan, Alice in her Wonderland. The wonderful Mickey Mouse waving the magic wand, casting us under his magical spell!

I remember crying in happiness, my dreams, my idols, here in front of me, delighting us with a world full of enchantment. My heart soared with the wonder of what we had seen. To this day I still feel that magic, locked up safe and warm in my adult heart. Waiting till I am asleep to come alive in my dreams.

What I add here must be said as it is a significant moment about how dreams can be made to come true. Across on the other side of the parades path stood a group of children, a group I'd say who were here on a make a wish type holiday. I can't say what illnesses they had; I can't even say who they were as individuals. As a child I only remember a lot of the children having no hair, and instantly relating that to how they were not very well. Not knowing how long they would not be well for. As a child I saw this and realised the sadness of the situation. But looking at their faces they looked anything but sad. They were just children, like me and all the other children there. Seeing their dreams come true in front of them. Feeling happiness stronger than most people had felt in their entire lives. The Disney characters on the ground took a child in their hands and danced with them in the parade. These children were special. They were strong and brave and deserved to have their every dream come true. These children must have felt so much pain but they were not angry or bitter. They were happy, that the time they had was being filled with their dreams coming true.

I don't know how long they had lived after this. But I can only hope they were happy, and surrounded by the people who loved them.

Later that night there was a firework display, the biggest I had ever seen. When the fireworks ended we saw a light in the distance, I thought it was a stray firework but as I looked closer I realised the light was human shaped. A woman flying through the air! Tinker bell. Tinker bell, here, now, flying through the air. It had to be her, people can't fly! It was her. The most magical sight I had ever seen! I still remember it to this day. All my dreams had come true, and even though I have gotten older, the magic has not dimmed. It's still there, in that childish side we keep hidden in our mind. Unseen but very much there.

2

Once, when we were children, my sister and I decided we had, had enough of living at home and would run away. We were going to run away to grans. We had packed little suitcases full of teddies, (no clothes or food.) We knew gran would clothe and feed us and she would be very happy to do that so we didn't need anything else.

We walked out the door and down the street, just two little girls walking hand in hand with our little suitcases. Mum was getting worried for us but dad was quite certain we would come back after a few steps with our tails between our legs. The further we got though he became less confident. A neighbour across the road walked over to him as he saw a five year old and a three year old walking down the street alone.

"You know your daughters are leaving?"

"Yes. They think they are running away, but they will be back soon" my dad said.

"Ah, I see."

We kept on walking . . . quickly reaching the end of the street.

"Any minute now they will turn back."

We had rounded the corner till we were no longer in sight.

"Shit!" Dad began running down the path after us. Unbeknown to him I had stopped us round the corner to reassess the situation. Our demands were clearly not being met and I didn't fancy walking all the way to grans when it was nearly lunch time. My little sister on the other hand was quite determined to carry on and make our parents suffer for some injustice we decided they must have done to us.

I managed to convince her that maybe running away wasn't the best solution right now and we should just go home for lunch and try again once we had eaten. She must have agreed and we began walking back down the street just as dad caught up with us.

We were soon grounded, received a slap on the backside and we did not get any lunch. Yes, Ffyona was right, we should have carried on to grans where we would have been fed six courses and spoilt rotten.

3

*'When I was 5 years old, my mother always told me
that happiness was the key to life. When I went to
school, they asked me what I wanted to be when I
grew up. I wrote down happy. They told me I didn't
understand the assignment. I told them they didn't
understand life.'*—John Lennon

My school days differed. I remember my first meeting
as a school councillor, deciding if we should create a
friendship garden and who we should perform as in the
school talent show, we chose Girls Aloud. I was Cheryl
Cole!

My teacher, Mr Brown, once brought in boxes of
Jaffa Cakes for us all. He made us sit down and be silent,
and we all waited patiently for what he was about to say
next. He slowly took out a Jaffa Cake from the box and
said, "Repeat after me, full moon." We all burst into fits
of giggles. If you know the old Jaffa Cake advert you will
understand the joke. We had to repeat what he said whilst
he continued to eat the delicious biscuit . . . cake . . .
things, we soon grew jealous that he was enjoying these
tasty treats and not giving us any. We begged for some
and he laughed and said no. As we began plotting our
Jaffa Cake heist he relented and let us all have one. Best
Jaffa Cake I ever had!

I remember once writing a story about a white tiger. This tiger lived in the forest, hiding from poachers, waiting patiently for the day when she could come out of hiding and be safe and accepted in the world. I was told to go to the headmistress, Mrs Reynolds, as she wanted to talk to me. I was scared that I was about to get into trouble but instead she congratulated me on my story and gave me a head teachers award. The award was a sticker but it was still quite a prestigious award for primary school.

The days I would sit under the blossom tree, wondering what my future would be like, you know as seven year olds do. I would also read National Geographic magazine, as seven year olds do. The teachers would bring in a box of magazines; there would be wedding magazines, car magazines and just one National Geographic. Of course the girls went for the wedding magazines to look at the pretty dresses, boys for the cars. Me, the random one in the class, wanting to travel and see the world!

Writing stories and researching history projects. Singing hymns every morning and Christmas songs in December.

I got the lead as Sandy in the Christmas play, a play that mixed Grease with Jack and the Beanstalk. With appearances by Del Boy and Rodney from Only Fools and Horses. This was the best time for me as I loved and still love Christmas, of course being a main part in a school play helped.

We made decorations for the classrooms and filled the hall with tinsel and glitter. I would walk past the Christmas tree when I was on an errand and would just delay my journey for a few seconds whilst I smelt the pine and looked at the baubles. I would always feel so much happier after that.

It wasn't always so wonderful however. A girl, who bullied me throughout primary school would kick and punch me repeatedly. She once pulled me by my hair right down to the ground; she soon stopped when my mum got her by the hair instead.

One time I caught a group of girls from my class going through my coat pockets. Later on in the day my friend came to me to say that some of my things had been put down the drain. I went to investigate and found my little toys staring back up at me in the dirt.

I recall feeling alone often. So much of my time was spent walking round the playground, watching the children play. Feeling so odd and alien to the world. In truth I was. I was odd, I was different. But it wasn't until I had grown up that I realised being different was so much better than being the same. I can't explain how, I will not bore you with words of wisdom about how it's good to be different. But they were all so similar. So like each other. Their names should have been child number one, child number two. It would not have made much difference. At least I was strange child number one and only! I had an identity. A strange one, but unique.

Our last play, which our school put on every year, was about what we wanted to be when we grew up. A red carpet had been set up and we would dress as our chosen professions and walk down to show off who we wanted to become. I wore my mums red dress, high heel shoes, and held a plastic Oscar award my teacher Miss Crossley had given me. Yes, I wanted to be an actress! It's strange to think that ten years on, it is still the career I dream about. I haven't changed at all, and Miss Crossley told me that if

I should ever be on stage making my Oscar speech I must mention her immediately! Well Miss Crossley I don't know if that will ever happen but I hope this is something at least.

I walked out of school feeling ready for the next step. I had met the most wonderful teachers who had helped me gain confidence. I had learnt a great deal and I had years' worth of memories. Some good, some not so good. But all these memories help to shape who you will be today.

4

High school felt like an alien universe. The school had one set of rules and the pupils had another. You have to be on both sides and do what each team asks you to do. By being more on one side you either become the little geek or the total tosser. You suddenly develop a personality disorder. With no hope of a cure until you decide to be brave and stop trying to impress everyone.

At age twelve my friends were drawing picture storyboards about what they would like to do with guys. They would draw what sex positions they wanted to try and write where each scenario would take place. At the time it seemed normal, but looking back, it was so wrong for us, so young and naive to be talking about sex! But that's what half of school was about. Sex. When you would and how you would. The scary truth is that we are getting younger and knowing more than we should.

Unfortunately I doubt that will get any better. I knew girls who believed that to get a new house or to get away from a parent they argued with was to get pregnant, have the baby, and in return they would be given a house and benefits by the council. I wish I could be making that up, I really do. As I got older in school one girl told me that she hated where she lived and hated her family, she wanted to get out. She then joked that getting 'preggers' would do that for her. It turned out that a year after we left school, she was pregnant, in her new house. Leaving the child with whomever she could, so she could go out and party.

That's what we have turned into, and I don't say that about every mum. Many genuinely want children and love them more than anything in the world. These mothers deserve everything they can get. But soon they may disappear behind a generation who aren't so loving and affectionate.

I sank into the routine of school as an anchor sinks to the sea bed. I felt grown up learning new things every day. Having to be responsible for myself was a scary prospect but also an exciting one.

5

I was now fifteen years old. I had friends who cared and lessons that were always enjoyable. My looks had relatively improved and I was happy. But most importantly, I had fallen in love. Yes I said it, love. You may be thinking that is too young, it's not love. Maybe it was just an immature, naive kind of love.

I will call him Jake for this. Jake wasn't particularly handsome. He wasn't Romeo, Mr Darcy or Edward Cullen. He was very funny though, very cheeky and very charming. I can't tell you exactly what drew me to him. My personality just instantly connected to his. Everything he said and did I was drawn too. My mind was consumed with thoughts of him. I persistently wondered how he was and what he might be doing. I imagined times we spent together and made up situations that hadn't even happened. I always hoped he thought about me as much as I thought about him.

Almost every day we would talk with one another and each time he asked me to be his. My dreams had come true.

There was a problem however, he had dated my best friend, and the first rule of friendship is to never go out with your best friends ex. It's one of them laws apparently written in the stars somewhere, and if broken would bring down upon you the harsh fires of hell. But through my sarcasm you must agree it's not good. Your best friend going out with your ex, how wrong is that! It is really, so I waited, in the hope that one day she would not care. I didn't want to hurt her but I knew I was also hurting myself.

"You are very sweet to wait for me." I said to him.

"No I'm stupid is there a difference?"

"Oh ok fine, don't wait, bog off!"

I ran away pretending to be annoyed, he chased after me and grabbed hold of waist. Tickling my sides and lifting me back towards him.

"You were running away from me!"

"Ha! Well attempting too, you tickled me that's cheating!"

"Well how else was I going to make you stop?"

"True." I freed myself from him and turned my gaze to his. "Thank you for waiting."

"Yeah, well, you can make up for it soon can't you." I picked up the sexual tone and tried to swat him in some form of chastise. He hopped away from me in a kind of backward, kangaroo jump. I stared at him in bewilderment as he made his small journey. After he stopped I stared at him perplexed. He looked back at me with the same confusion. After a few seconds we both began to laugh. We laughed so hard I felt my stomach begin to hurt. In this moment I felt more love for this boy than I ever thought possible.

How stupid of me. Weeks later he was going out with Rebecca. Some slut he knew that I decided was a slut even though she may have been quite nice. But I felt devastated. This was my Jake. My Jake with this girl, this stupid, inconvenient girl! I was hurting. Hurting so much I thought my heart would break apart from the rending pain I felt every time my thoughts strayed to him.

But should I have been angry? I had asked him to wait but he had his own life, his own desires and his own happiness to think about. He signed no oath. He made no promises. But the pain hurt like a knife wound inside me and I decided I wasn't going to feel like this ever again. I was going to delete him from my memory. Not an easy thing to do for your first love.

Within a few weeks he had broken up with that silly girl and began flirting with me again. I didn't want to feel that hurt again, I wanted to forget all about him. It was difficult though. Half of me said 'Who cares?' the other half was saying, "You do stupid". I needed time that was all.

We all have that friend who has all the cool parties and knows all the cool people and this friend usually lives in the house of love. As all relationships or 'flirtationships' begin in that house. Most of the party was spent trying to get two young people together. Can you guess who? Yes me and my Jake, the Jake I hoped I could forget about.

Sometime during the party I got cornered between the walls of the house, with my two friends on both sides and Jake standing in front of me. They said how we needed to 'go out' and would not let me leave until I said yes, repeating to me the same devastating commands. Jake stared at me with eyes only Puss in Boots should get away with, waiting for me to say yes of course I will! I continued to explain that I wasn't sure. I needed time to think, to establish my feelings. This guy had hurt me and I was trying to block him from my mind.

But they were staring at me, waiting for me to answer with only one particular word, I was trapped. I said yes. I shouldn't have but I did. I spent the whole night feeling foolish for not being brave. Not asking for space to think. I should have stood up for myself.

As the summer progressed, I had a lot of time on my hands to think about this situation I had got myself into. I wasn't happy. I knew that for certain. I had let myself be pushed into something I hadn't been sure about. I decided I didn't want to be with him. So you know what I did, I did something truly awful, the only thing you should not do when breaking up with someone. Break up text. Yes I sent him a text saying it was over. It wasn't nice but I was young. I wouldn't dream of such a thing now, but back then I thought it didn't matter. I made that decision, not realising at the time that it would come to be the biggest regret of my life so far. I hurt him more than I could have thought possible, and the arguments we had were truly prize worthy.

But as time passed he learnt to forgive me and we began to speak again. We would flirt and talk like we use too, and that is when I realised the awful mistake I had made, how stupid I had been. I was more in love with him than ever, and I had ruined it all.

Two days before Christmas I logged in on MSN, ready to talk to my Jake. He was online, and he was with his new girlfriend. Another stab through my heart. This time I blamed myself. I felt it was my fault; I deserve this for hurting him. I had ended things in the first place; it was the consequence of the mistake I had made.

He spoke to me for a while and then his girlfriend and I were left to chat. She told me about a lovely 'jump on the bed' they had. It was such a ridiculous way to put it, but it had hit its mark. That bitch had been with him. When it should have been with me! The time he spent with her, all along was meant to be the time he should have spent with me. But it was my fault. I had hurt him first.

That Christmas I was so distraught. I couldn't enjoy myself and I went to bed that night crying myself to sleep. Silly girl, you had only yourself to blame. By the end of the year he was no longer with her and we renewed our toxic bond. He would rarely say anything romantic or kind. But when he did I felt drunk, high, addicted to any affection he could give.

Soon he was with someone else. Each time my hopes would be raised and then destroyed. Each time I blamed myself. Until the seventh time, (give or take) I realised, I hurt him once. He's hurt me many, many times over. I don't deserve this anymore. I won't blame myself for this again.

We would never work and never will. I must move on. My friends would joke how we were like Ross and Rachel from 'Friends'. He would say to me that we will end up together. No matter what we do it will always be us in the end. I believed him. But that was such a silly dream. I would cry, forcing myself not to think about him. It was such sweet torture. Imagining times between us, times that would never happen. Sometimes I was so miserable; thinking about him was the only thing that would get me through the day. Like taking heroin, I knew I shouldn't take more but I couldn't stop either.

6

We went to London on a school trip and I can't tell you how excited I was. We went to see the Houses of Parliament and Big Ben, which isn't really that big when you see it in person. But as my dad pointed out to me Big Ben isn't actually the clock it's the bell inside, so I'm sure that's very big and therefore its reputation can be maintained.

It was so fantastic to see the place where decisions have been made about my countries welfare for hundreds of years. We walked into an incredibly large hall, which was very old as some of the oldest decisions were made here. The tour guide gathered us into a semi-circle around him and told us that a particularly famous person was tried there in the very spot he stood. He said he would give us a clue and told us he was Scottish. Well the geek side of me decided to have an epileptic fit. I stretched out my arm and actually uttered the words, "Ooh, ooh." Hand waving in the air and feet stretching upwards, the guide looked at me and laughed.

"Yes, you?" he asked me.

"WILLIAM WALLACE!" I yelled. He laughed at me and said I was right to which my friend whispered to me, "God you're such a nerd." Yes maybe I am a little.

Next we took a tour round the National Theatre. I was surprised to see how modern it was. I expected a

Victorian, gothic building, with chandeliers and red carpets everywhere.

We visited the room where War Horse was being prepared for a show that very night. We were taken round the room and brought onto that stage. Here I was reader, standing on a stage in the National Theatre. I felt such a profound sensation settle over me. Suddenly in that moment I felt such exhilaration. Such excitement and happiness. Oh if I could be here always! The stage is the real home to so many actors out there. The place they can truly become themselves.

It is strange reader, strange that the only time I am truly myself, is when I am on stage pretending to be somebody else.

We watched some west end shows. Wicked I have to say was my favourite. I cried just hearing Idina Menzel hit the notes, making the songs sound so powerful.

Before we left, our drama teacher asked us where we would like to go to eat. We all agreed on Chinese, and this is where we all made a mistake. When we said Chinese, what we actually meant was fish and chips from the local 'chippy'. We instead walked into a thoroughly oriental restraunt that served real Chinese food. A few of us took advantage to try something new, however a great many of the girls decided instead, to complain and bitch about the evening. It was our own fault; we had made assumptions and were being taught a lesson. We were so ignorant and some of the class didn't even try the food to see if they liked it or not.

We watched a trial in the Old Bailey, something I was very excited about as I love law and criminology. I must admit I was expecting some kind of murderer being tried, instead we got some small issue that bored us to tears and all of us were taking it in turns to pinch the person next to us when they started dozing. We didn't even see the other person in the trial, so in our point of view it was incredibly one sided.

7

Jake and I, we . . . we had our first kiss. I know I was trying to forget him but every time I see his face the rational thoughts disappear from my mind, and are replaced by silly, hopeless romantic ones.

We were at the house of love again, playing spin the bottle. I know not exactly romantic, and not exactly moving on. I didn't care though I was too excited. The bottle had pointed at me, and was now being spun again. I looked around the circle hoping it would land on the one person I had tactically avoided looking at throughout the game. It stopped. It was pointing to the person directly in front of me. Jake, when I saw it land on him I thought my heart would explode in my chest. He stood up and held his hand out towards me. I looked down at this hand. His hand. Do I really take this risk? Before my brain could rationalise what my body was doing, I had raised my hand towards his, and took hold.

We walked out of the room, for some form of privacy, and went into the kitchen.

Oh god! Jake, my Jake, he looked at me and smiled. I felt my lips tremble in anticipation, was this really happening?

"Are you okay?" He asked me smiling.

"Fine." My voice responded cracking.

"You really don't know how long I have wanted to do this."

"Me too."

He smiled at my response. "I fucking love you." His hand moved towards my waist. Hell how was I not fainting right now! My whole body felt like jelly, going weaker I suddenly forgot how to hold myself up. I gripped onto the table for support as he grabbed hold of my waist.

"I don't know why." I said slowly.

"What do you mean you don't know why?"

"I don't know why you would love me, I'm mad, and I'm difficult I'm . . ."

"You may be mad and difficult but you are a mad, difficult woman I love."

He looked into my eyes, and I gazed into his. Those blue eyes, those lush lips, he could tell me to walk through fire and I would. My body felt like it was on fire! His head moved towards me. I shook with excitement and a slight twinge of fear. A kiss, his kiss, finally everything felt so perfect.

His lips touched mine, a shock of adrenaline rushed through my body. My head naturally tilted to one side as my arms reached around his neck. Hot and cold chills moved through me, I couldn't help but to clasp myself closer to him, he responded even more passionately.

His fingers ran across my back, through my hair. He stopped for a second to look into my eyes. I stared back into his with love and longing, such aching longing. A moan escaped his lips before he locked onto mine and kissed me again. His kiss turned violent, even more beautiful than before. A shudder escaped the enclosure of my skin as I pressed my body into his. I love you.

Someone had walked in and we moved our heads away. He smiled at me and took hold of my hand again. Don't let this end Jake, don't hurt me.

Of course he hurt me. He has and continues too. It would hurt to think about him, but not thinking about him caused me even more pain. Thinking of him just made me delusional. I felt a fake sense of happiness. It was like getting high of a drug. It felt so good, and when I needed that boost, I had to take it. Not taking it brought me to the harsh reality, and I was not strong enough to face that. No, it's better to just pretend. Live in a dream and pretend real life wasn't the reality. How weak have I become?

Eventually I saw the change though. After the constant dreaming and complaining to friends, and near enough stalking him with my thoughts I gradually saw what he was becoming. He was changing into a horrible person. Drugs and sex were nothing. He became something I was repulsed by. A bad influence my grandma might have said. He was truly the bad boy now, and to correct the ideas guys have about girls going for only the bad boys, it isn't true. He wasn't a bad boy when I fell for him; I was still in love with the boy he used to be. He had just changed the outfit, and I tried to look past it for something better. The boy had gone though. He disappeared the day I sent him that text. It wasn't until four years later; I read a quote in a book that would kill those poisoned feelings forever.

'You loved a memory and that can be one of the most powerful forms of love. In memory, all faults are stripped away, and all that is left is a reflection off your own divine; Perfection, a dream.'—Jules Watson, The White Mare.

In essence, I was in love with someone who did not exist anymore. I was in love with a dream. Why be with someone who isn't the person you loved. Who didn't really treat you like the princess you deserve to be treated as. Something that truly did not exist. These little sentences proved to be a lesson I would never forget. I was soon what you may call 'over him'. There may always be that soft spot. But I will never be in danger of falling for him again. For a time I felt hard and bitter. But heartbreak is a good lesson. It teaches you not to make the same mistakes again. To realise that you can find someone better suited to you. Why spend so much time with someone who's so wrong for you and who you are so wrong for too. You think, you cry, you get back up and you begin again. Isn't that what every situation in life is about? Learning, correcting, living.

I was finally over him. But I was scared and uncomfortable with the idea of relationships. By now I was too comfortable with being on my own. You can't miss what you've never had. I hadn't had a guy hold me and tell me it would be okay. I was fine. Fine.

My dream world would say otherwise. Of course there's nothing wrong with dreaming. I would imagine situations between us. I would imagine situations between a number of people. With Jake it would make me feel better in a rough time.

Even now, I like to imagine having someone there for me in some form. Some faceless man, always there in spirit. You will think I'm crazy. I think I'm just lonely. Maybe both are similar.

Maybe a crazy fantasy isn't loneliness. It could be hope. Hope for . . . hope for some change. Welcome relief from the cold side of the bed. Hope for someone to argue with. Hope for someone to laugh with. The hope of not being so alone anymore. Alone . . . Am I really so alone?

8

We were spending two weeks in France. We had rented a farmhouse next to the woods. I don't remember too much about what it looked like. I did think it was magical though. The garden overlooked some hills, and I can still remember seeing the mist evaporate from the trees in the warm, morning sun. Everything felt alive and fresh, the country was waking up, preparing for a new day.

In the early days of the holiday we discovered that living near the house, somewhere in the woods, lived a group of wild kittens. They would play in the garden every morning, whilst we watched them from the kitchen window.

One day I walked outside to see if there was any chance they would come running up to me and want to play. Obviously they didn't and ran away. I was stubborn though, I wanted them to know I wouldn't hurt them. So every day I sat outside on the step and waited.

Every day for hours I waited near, sitting patiently, watching them as they played. Eventually they became more comfortable with my presence and even got curious. One of the kittens, who was the bravest or cockiest of the family decided to take the initiative and investigate me. He walked up to me as bold as brass and climbed up onto my lap. Well that was it; that was all we needed.

Every day my kittens would sit with me and play. We would put out bowls of milk and any tins of tuna we could find for them. They were utterly adorable, but most importantly they were my friends. I was only eleven at the time and I thought life was pretty perfect.

My little kitten, the brave, cocky one, would always stay with me. I have always been a dog person but I loved this little cat. I loved him so much.

I guess here I learnt about how intimately the good and bad parts of life can mix together. How suddenly life can alter itself without warning.

Every day I spent, waiting so patiently for my kitten and the others to feel safe with me. Waiting and finally earning their trust. Being able to feed and play with them, and feel so utterly happy.

Then it all ended. We had decided to go into the village near the house; we had stopped at the end of the driveway whilst we waited for a car to drive past. All of a sudden my dad told us not to look at the road. Of course we were going to look. That's when we saw him, my kitten, spread on the road, bloodied and ripped apart. I was devastated. I was only a child, and seeing this beautiful little kitten like that, seeing death so blatantly put out before me, I realised how cruel life could be. How it didn't care if you were small, tall, good, bad, young or old. If it picked on you, then that was it. There was nothing you could do.

9

"Annabella will you come with me."

"Yes Mrs Roache" It wasn't a question it was a kind command. I hadn't done anything wrong as far as I was aware.

"Tuck your shirt in." Crap.

"Yes miss", I replied. We walked down the studio steps, the corridors were absent from noisy school children. I truly loved my school. Its teachers kind and supportive, the building a comfortable, secure place in my life. We arrived at the Pastoral office. My teacher looked at me then walked in. Being a drama teacher she was prone to making dramatic entrances. Being a terrific actress and a crazy but kind teacher no one minded. I followed her in, where my head of year was waiting for me. She greeted me with a smile and said she had something to tell me.

"You know of course Annabella in the last year we pick students who have done well and deserve to be a prefect to represent the school. Well we have decided we want you as a prefect. Not only that, but as you know we have the new school houses, red, yellow, green and blue. We will have a head prefect for each house and we want you to be head prefect for yellow house." At this point I was on the floor in a pool, so you can imagine what I was like at the next part.

"And as you will know, every year we select a head boy and girl for their year. The vote was unanimous; we want you to be our next head girl." Before I knew it I was crying and hugging my teachers. When asked how I felt the only word I was able to produce was 'cool'. Not my finest thank you speech but I was in shock. They asked me if I wanted to phone my parents and tell them. I picked up the phone and dialled. I know this day to be a Wednesday. How I know is because my mum was off work on Wednesdays and my dad took his day off on the same day so he could be with her.

"Mum I have something to tell you." She burst into tears when I repeated the words just spoken to me. She said I had to tell dad, after I did he was also crying. I reluctantly put the phone down and turned round to my teachers. Both were beaming at me.

Mrs Roache handed me a tin of biscuits and told me to take one. I took a chocolate digestive and tried to savour this moment just as my mouth savoured the chocolate on my tongue.

"You can't tell anyone now you have to keep it to yourself." What! I couldn't tell a soul about this extraordinary moment! Lonely, weird, innocent little Annabella. Chosen for Head girl, out of everyone ME! Happiness exploding through me and having to pretend nothing had happened.

Mrs Roache told me to relax and we could go back into class. I composed myself and walked out of the room, my drama teacher treading next to me. She told me I would really need to use my drama skills now.

We entered the drama studio and the class looked at me. I walked to my group and carried on with the scene. They asked me what had happened and I told them it was about an exam I will miss because of a school trip. They quickly lost interest and went back to work. I looked back at Mrs Roache and we shared a secret smile. It was the proudest day of my life.

10

My sister Ffyona and I were at our grandma's house. Grandma's friend, Eunice, was sitting next to me on the sofa, asking me how my day was at school. I answered her timidly; still very shy not really knowing what to say to her. The phone rang and my grandma got up to answer it. The only phone was located in the hallway, near the front door. My grandad had 'The Bill' on, a police show I was fascinated with at the time. Probably because I thought I could act in it one day.

Breaking the comfortable buzz of the television my grandma suddenly screamed out. My grandad rushed to the lounge door and slammed it open, my grandma, after what felt like hours, came back in crying. She collapsed on to the sofa weeping and moaning. Eunice pleaded with her to tell her what was wrong. The words she said I remember so clearly, "They got my boy, they got my boy". After, I remember sitting on the stairs holding on to Ffyona. Both of us crying with fear.

We knew that boy was our big brother Jonathan, we knew that much. The rest we weren't too sure about. I held on to my little sister, holding her so tightly I hoped to hug away her pain and fear into me. My memory stops there. What I found out later goes like this. Jon, my beautiful brother, had gone to the shop near our home, on a warm, sunny afternoon wanting to buy a paper and a chocolate bar. Nothing unusual for him, an almost weekly tradition.

Before he reached the shop however a gang of young thugs attacked him.

I know they battered him to the ground. Kicking him repeatedly, jumping and standing on him. A neighbour opened the door and asked what was going on; he saw my brother on the floor, with the thugs around him. My brother screamed for the man to help him. The neighbour simply walked back into his house, and shut the door.

One of them jumped on his head, jumping so hard it left a shoe imprint on his forehead for weeks afterwards. They left him. Bloodied and battered. He had crawled his way the short distance home, with no one attempting to help him. He fell against the door and cried.

Dad held him, shouting at him to tell him which way they had gone. Jon managed to point in a general direction and dad threw him on to my mum. His words went something like, "I'm going to kill the bastards". He phoned his brothers and they all went on a hunt after the thugs. My mum phoned for an ambulance. My brother desperately just wanted to sleep, my mum was told to slap him to keep him awake, that under no circumstances must he fall asleep. She sobbed having to slap him repeatedly round the face to keep him awake. He nearly died that day.

Bastards. I want to kill the Bastards who hurt my beautiful, brave brother. Those bastards had attacked a few more lads that day. One of them had been beaten like Jon; another had been attacked with a makeshift bat with nails sticking through it. Another had been slit from ear to ear.

However they were never caught. We had CID working with us, who did everything they could. They had extra units and worked extra time to catch them. It just didn't happen. I only blame them bastards.

They didn't care about how many lives they destroyed, how long another human being would suffer for their actions. The brain damage done to my brother was terrible; he suffers with problems now and will for the rest of his life.

He is still the kind, gentle person he has always been though. He will help anyone and will always try his best to make us smile. He is a truly beautiful soul, so I'd hope you understand the anger I feel when I say quite freely that I hope those bastards will one day go to hell. But for now my brother will live that hell for them, for the rest of his life. More than ten years has passed since then. My brother still hurts. I wonder if they feel the guilt. Do they feel sorry for what they did? I think that they probably do not.

11

Ever had such a brilliant day with your friends, a day filled with so much fun and laughter, but somewhere deep inside your brain there is a little voice of knowledge telling you that this kind of day will never happen again?

One such day, myself and my friends went to the park, carrying baskets filled with crisps, and sandwiches. Bottles of coke and juice and stacks of chocolate bars and biscuits. The sun was shining and the Manchester temperatures were positively tropical.

We exited the busy tram and filed across the road into Heaton Park. We found a patch of grass and set out our blankets. We stuffed our mouths with the treats and talked about the end of term and the amazing summer we were about to have. One friend pulled out a guitar, and we all chanted along to Songbird by Oasis. It was a rare moment shared between a group of people, knowing how happy we all were to be together. How grateful we felt for what we had in our lives.

The guys had a game of football which my friend Hannah and I joined in with. Later on, a small group of us went through the woods to the back of the duck pond. Or a small lake rather, as it had mini canoe boats gliding through it. My best friends Dan and Dane got straight into the water, soon pushing me into it as well. Being a duck lake/pond it wasn't the cleanest of places to go for a random swim. There was also the big question of is this actually legal what we are doing, swimming in this place used for boats and the local wildlife? The answer was probably no.

Being young though it didn't stop us. It wasn't until I got home that I realized how perfect the day was, and how it would probably be the last outing we as that group of friends would ever have. In hindsight it was. We never went back to that park together, and the group outings never happened again. It is sad how good times can never last forever, but the bad times can. One day was all we had, and plans to repeat it were never made. It seems bittersweet to think about the way we were. What we had. If I had known my days would get darker, I would have made that day last longer. Much longer.

12

I was bullied, quite badly in my last year of school. The bully was a friend, a best friend once. The ones we trust can also be the ones who hurt and betray us the most.

The friend began to distance herself from her normal circle of friends, including me. She began to change, and I decided I would just have to accept that as life. She started name calling my family. Particularly my mum. This I would not accept.

Let me explain my mum to you very quickly. She is a beautiful woman, of course I will be biased, but she truly is. She has big green eyes and brown curly hair. She left school when she was sixteen and went straight into work. She met a man who liked to wine and dine her. Buying her expensive things and taking her out to expensive places. He was charming and handsome. Mum was completely smitten, but that would soon end. He beat her one day, she was devastated but she was not going to be used as a punch bag. She ended things but found out some months later that she was pregnant. She decided to keep the baby. That baby would turn out to be my big brother Jonathan. She has always and is still facing battles. But she is brave, and incredibly strong. This in particular makes me proud to be her daughter.

She makes Christmas dinners for old men and women whose families don't even visit them at that time of year or even give them a dinner of their own.

She once worked at a care home. She firmly believes to this day you should never die alone. So when her old ladies or gents were near the end, she would be called in (by her own orders) and stay with them, till they took their last breath. She finds amusement in the smallest things and can be quite ditsy when she's happy. My mum will be nice to you, if you are nice to her.

The friend continued to bad mouth her. If she had stopped at this however I would have been happier. But like an evil bitch, or maybe just a woman. (Yes, sorry I am a woman too.) She had to go a bit further. It seems like harmless name calling but I need you to know the mental damage it would soon do.

As time went on the name calling and bullying was directed at me. Our small group of friends began separating. I was slowly being pushed out, and made to feel it was my fault. A place I felt at home became difficult and awkward. Being a young, silly girl, I was still at the teen point believing friends were more important than family. It seemed like everyone had turned cold and tired of me. I was grasping on to strings that were slowly been dragged out from my fingers. Isolated was a good way to describe how I felt. I blamed myself constantly. They wouldn't be doing this if I was better, more normal, more . . . Well not me.

Eventually I had apparently done things with guys. Now that may not seem like the worst thing to say, but to me it was. It was because I was so innocent. Innocent where boys were concerned anyway. My mum once told me that when she was young she was walked home by a guy she knew. They talked and he dropped her off at the doorstep and then left. Nothing more. When my mum got into school the next day however she was the class slut. She had apparently done it with the guy and also cheating on her boyfriend in the process. My mum had done none of this, but a girl isn't believed in this situation. It's true when they say if a girl does these 'things', she is a slag. When a guy does though he's the hero! Even worse if the girl didn't do anything to receive the name in the first place.

I was also scared. I once heard my dad talking about a party he went to when he was younger. He had gone upstairs to the bathroom and found a queue forming. He thought this was the line to the bathroom. When this line didn't seem to be moving too quickly though he went to investigate what it was. Apparently a girl had been given some form of drug and as she lay drunk and disorientated on the bed, the boys in the line were taking turns with her. I think you can guess what they were doing on their turns. I was disgusted by what I had heard and after listening to both stories I promised myself not to go anywhere near the subject of sex whilst I was in school.

I know it seems like a tricky promise to keep but I did it. I wasn't going to be hurt or disrespected. I was too afraid to trust anyone anyway. After school I would do what I wanted, however now I was just going to learn and carefully end my childhood.

But as rumours spread I became the dark horse, this not so good girl slut. It was so easy for people to believe it however. We all like to believe the worst of others. Even better if it is a good girl gone bad. If the bad girl does something wrong, it's no shock. In fact it's expected. But imagine the timid girl, the geek, who once cried when she got into trouble, is actually a little slut, who will do it with anyone and everyone, the nice girl who isn't so nice. What would you think? A part of you may question, however a large part might go, 'Oh my, she kept that hidden!' You might joke about it with your friends. When you walk past her, wondering if you will see her as the dark horse she's concealed so well. I know this because I've done this too. Instantly thought the worst of someone. Even if their character said otherwise. I've done it. Many people I know had. Maybe it was my lesson, my turn. I was being called the worst thing I could possibly be called. But not only was it being said. It was being believed.

The loyalties of my friendships were questioned and it turned out only a handful actually believed me. Even a smaller handful stood by me. At this time I was also playing my role as head girl. This made it worse because not only was the good girl bad, the head girl was. I knew that once tagged as this slut that guys may think I would be an easy catch. One guy in a drunken text asked me if he could 'screw the head girl'. Others later told me they did all sorts to try and be head girls first. I was like a prize to be won, a trophy for that guy. I must stress to you reader that I do not mean this in the, 'I'm beautiful' sense of having that trophy of a girl. It was simply getting the girl that didn't put out. The girl that was and had to be good because she was the head girl.

People would send me abusive texts and e-mails. Phoning me; whispering and laughing at the other end. Eventually every time the phone rang I was too terrified to answer it. My friends were cornered in rooms and intimidated. My little sister was at the school also, and I didn't want to confront them, for fear they would get at her instead. They never did but that fear stayed with me for the whole year.

This continued on days out with my family. One sunny day I was at the park with my grandma and they sent me abusive texts. I instantly felt scared and distraught. I lived in fear that they would come to the house and hurt me there.

Can you see the mental damage being inflicted? It turns out it caused a lot more damage than I thought. I got ill, as in mentally ill. A word I was afraid to say for so long. But I had to say it to myself sometime. Depression. It is difficult to describe depression unless you have had it yourself. I will tell you more about this but for now I should just like to make you aware of the reasons for it.

Several times I walked to the school office to give up my role as head girl. My G.C.S.E's were only weeks away, was I really going to go through with them. Was I going to be able to deal with the mental illness I had developed, and also handle the pressure of prefect roles and important life altering exams? I could fail. I could do so terribly all because of these people.

Thinking back I don't know how I did it. I don't know how many times I managed to find the strength to carry on. I just did.

I remember several times sat by the side of my bed, with the scissors against my wrist. Willing myself to force the blade down into my skin and drag it across. So many times wondering if it would distract me from the pain I felt inside. The dark bottomless pit of pain I felt, that wouldn't disappear. I hated my life, myself, this pathetic creature curled up in a ball on the floor, holding the scissors against her wrist, wondering who would truly miss her. I would throw the scissors away from me each time. Not finding the strength to do it. Something inside me saying no you're better than that, don't do this. I got up to go to school every morning. Coming home every evening. Acting so well my parents never noticed the problem.

I realised my one sanctuary fell to only three factors. My family, my books and drama. Every week I went to my drama club and escaped into a completely different world. In acting I could be anyone I wanted to be. Annabella, school girl and mentally ill weirdo did not exist. The strange lonely creature had disappeared. I could be Laura or Amy or Juliet! They were all different people with a different set of problems. My problems could disappear into some others. Some problems I could deal with. A character with a better life than my own.

My books allowed me to escape into the beautiful, fantasy worlds. If I could I would thank people like JK Rowling, Christopher Paolini, Jane Austen and Charles Dickens. Authors of books that inspired me to dream and escape. To take my mind away from the misery being inflicted upon it.

Also my family of course. Always helping me to smile and laugh when times were so dark and miserable.

The school I loved became a place I hated to be at. The teachers gave me some relief and for that I could never thank them enough. Mr Gildea, Mrs Roache, Mr West and Mr Fisher who probably had to sink his teeth into his lips to keep himself silent when I told him I had ambitions on becoming an actress.

By the end of the year things seemed to brighten up. But I was left exhausted and deflated. I could get away from the friends who hurt me so much, but I would be left with some devastating after effects. Like a drug addict still feeling the effects of the cocaine leaving the body. Only, these effects would still be with me years on. To this day I still feel a slight fear when the phone rings. I will sometimes wake up at night crying at the re occurring dreams I've had since my last year in school. Also the mental illness, the depression, still working its way into my mind. Keeping me company all the time. Sometimes staying distant, other times making its presence known like a giant forest fire.

I would rock a lot. You know like back and forth. Looking like the stereotypical image of a mental patient in the films. Crying and rocking. Sometimes not realising I was doing it. I couldn't tell anyone my feelings. At a temperamental time of my life anyway, raging hormones entering my body, everything was bound to feel more dramatic than it was. I hoped so many times it was just that. But that would be pretending nothing had happened. That I felt no fear, no upset, no despair.

I couldn't even get up off the floor most of the time. Why bother, just stay here on this cold floor. Let me stay with it and keep it company. Let my existence fade away from the world's knowledge. Forgetting I was there. Let my pain disappear into my body; let my body disappear into the floor. Let the floor disappear into the earth. Swallowing us all up so that we never existed. Let it all just melt away.

At this time I had made the silly mistake of dating a friend, in the hope that I could be 'normal' again. He had to deal with the rumours too. Even the younger students asked him why his girlfriend had 'shagged' her friends crush. I soon broke up with him. He didn't deserve the crap being thrown at him. I was at this time still madly in love with Jake so I was being unfair again.

What the hell was happening? Here's a tip, never ask for an eventful life. You may regret what you wished for. When did I get so weak? How had I lowered myself to this? I'd never felt so empty and broken. I hope you never feel this, although in this world we have created for ourselves I'm sure you will at some point.

I will leave it there, I hope I haven't bored you too much, but it was such a dark year. Somehow I managed to pull myself through it. I didn't escape unscratched though. I handled it awfully in the sense that I couldn't let go. Not completely, not that I haven't tried. So long I wanted to delete the memories and feelings from my mind. Like a computer file or a text message. Escape the pain I have and do feel to this day. But it's not that easy, it never is. I will do the best I can, but that is all I can do.

13

Every year, since I was born, we would take a nine hour drive, usually three times a year, right up to the west highlands of Scotland. To a little fishing village called Aultbea. Aultbea once had only a few farm houses, a school house and a shop. The rest of the village was farm land and mountains. Five hundred years ago my great, great, (however many other greats later) grandfather, built a house on top of the hill, right next to the sea. Each new generation built on to it, making it the beautiful house it is today.

Five hundred years later, this beautiful farm house, with its beautiful white stone walls is my home. The barn that once housed the cows and coal stands empty. Hundred year old beams hold the oars from my great grandfather's boat. He was a fisherman. A dangerous job as it still is in today's fishing industry.

Being a little village, hidden away from the outside world, village life was also about survival. At one point the village was left with hardly any food. The local fishermen knew that they needed to get food for their wives and children. But the weather was fierce, and if they didn't survive neither would the village. They took a chance. They set out early one morning, packed supplies and said goodbye to their families. They then set off into their boats to begin the hunt. Horrible storms accompanied them, and a sudden violent wave tipped my great grandfathers boat, knocking him overboard. He was rescued by the other men, who managed to bring him back from the clutches of death. (He had told people that he felt peaceful, drowning in the churning mass of water and foam, and it was not as harsh as people thought it was.)

Days went by and as people began to give up hope a farm lad spotted something coming towards the beach. On closer inspection he realised it was the sails of the fishermen's boats. The boy ran to the nearest farm and soon the whole village had heard that the men were coming home. The men were reunited with their wives and children and I'm sure a lot of tears were shed. Fish was unloaded onto the beach and the village finally had the food they needed.

There are different types of heroics in the world but to feed an entire village, saving them from starvation. That is a truly heroic thing, and I feel proud that my great grandfather was a part of that.

My great grandmother would stand outside the kitchen window gutting the fish and peeling the potatoes. Carrying one child on her back, one round her front and another one on the floor next to her.

An image my mum always had of her grandmother was her sat beside the fire in her rocking chair, doing her knitting. When someone entered the house they would immediately be given food and a dram of whiskey. The rule being, no one leaves the house with an empty stomach, (or sober.) That is the rule for community life. Look after each other, help each other.

My grandma would tell me stories of child life in the village. She would walk the two miles to school every day, help to milk the cows and feed the chickens. Go to the local dances and dream one day of meeting her Prince Charming.

She also told me of the harsh times of isolated village life. My grandma spoke once about a woman a few farms away that had been diagnosed with cancer. She was in so much pain my grandma could hear her screams from over the next hill.

Life could also be lonely, being so isolated in the mountains. Especially if you were a young woman who wanted excitement and adventure!

So every year we go to this house and spend our holidays there. We meet our friends, Margaret-Ann and Dougie, Ken and Jean, my mum's oldest friend Angela and great aunt Dolly.

Looking out from the house you can see acres upon acres of farmland, with sheep and highland cattle grazing on it. In the spring, new born lambs run around next to their mothers, charging underneath them to drink the milk, their little tails wagging excitedly.

The mountains reach so high the tops are swallowed up by the clouds, like stepping stones up to the gods themselves. The ocean with shades of deep blue hails the sun's rays as they shimmer like diamonds onto the water. The breeze sails through the grass, reviving this, wild, beautiful land.

In this place I call my home; it feels like I have entered another world. A world where all the worries and problems of life just slip away. For once, all the sadness and darkness on earth is lifted, and this beautiful heaven is revealed. Through the dark depressed time I felt through my last year in school, I realised I needed Aultbea more then I needed food or water. For once my mind and my heart could escape from the darkness and pain I'd felt for so long.

I couldn't recognise who I was, but here I could see myself again. The world looked magical once more and I held onto this euphoric paradise as tight as I could. But the more I relaxed, the more I realised I couldn't stay here forever. I couldn't just run away as much as I wanted. I had to go back and face everything that had made me so sad for so long. I needed to face those dark times and hold my head up bloody high. I think at this point I realised I had grown up. Running away from bad situations is an easy thing to do. It's painless. Happier. The real difficult task is going back to that same dark prison, and fighting it head on. Standing up to the demons that haunted you for so long and saying 'Look at how strong I am, stronger than you will ever be.'

With this knowledge in my head I intended to build up my strength (mentally) and have a good time. Everyday me and my sister would walk down the small hill to the beach at the bottom. We named this our beach and even though it may not be legally I still state that it is our beach and always will be!

We would take a picnic and find our rock to sit on and eat. We had names for all the rock formations on our beach. There is a bit of rock that looks like 'Pride Rock' from The Lion King. There is also a secret part which I called My Haven. This is a flat piece of rock you could lie down on. It is surrounded by higher rocks and in the centre the water rolls in and makes a little secluded area. Here is where I would spend a great deal of time thinking and relaxing. It wasn't till my sister found me and completely invaded my haven that she then used it as her relaxation stop and christened it her haven as well.

When the weather was bad we would be confined to the indoors where books and puzzles were our only source of entertainment. Yes, no internet or game consoles either. I didn't half mind the simplicity of it though. Here I learnt the enjoyment of spending time with family, actually talking for a change. We would sit together in the kitchen laughing and joking. I would peel the potatoes for mum and end up peeling my fingers instead.

Once at dinner my dad was putting salt on his food as he usually did, but this time no salt was appearing. He blew on to the top of the salt pot and the bottom lid blew off, instantly pouring half a jar of salt onto his dinner. My dad sat there in shock staring at his ruined meal. But mum, Fe, Jon and I nearly spat out our food in helpless giggles. Dad was devastated but not wanting to waste his delicious dinner merely scraped it off and ate what he could.

We always go to Inverness for a shopping trip or take a twenty minute drive to the next nearest village from Aultbea. This village is called Gairloch. Here we always go to a garden centre and a little old book store. I happened to find a book that was over a hundred years old. Of course I bought it and hate to touch it now in case it falls apart.

There is a pub we go to and this pub is the true image of the real 'country pub'. The building is made from old white stone, with gothic windows and little doors. Trees overlook the structure and it is surrounded by a beautiful garden. A stream runs through the property with an old stone bridge built over the water. Under the bridge the stream runs its course to the harbour. At this harbour a seal called Sammy visits and waves at passing people, hoping for some fish.

The time we spend here it seems like the sun is always shinning. This might mean in a psychological aspect that I was always happy and enjoying myself. I could describe to you all day what this place is like. But I don't think I could even give it justice to how truly beautiful it is. The little house in Aultbea, with its history and happiness, the beautiful people who live near and the wonderful serenity it gives to everyone who sees it, is truly one of the most secret paradises on earth. Its magical wilderness would truly take your breath away. It does to me anyway.

14

I put on my beautiful prom dress. Made of a glistening red material, that would shimmer pink in the sunlight. The actual colour was valentine. This made me feel all the more pretty in it. The bottom part of the dress had pickups in the material which reminded me of Belle's dress in Disney's Beauty and the Beast. The bodice was tightly fitted, with black and silver diamantes in the middle scooping in a sweetheart neckline.

There aren't many times I can look in the mirror and tell myself that I look beautiful. But this time I really could. My hair was a mass of blonde curls. My make-up had been done by my mum's friend, Lisa, who had very much helped turn an ugly duckling into a swan. I stood in the mirror gazing at the beautiful person in front of me. Not quite believing it was really me. My grandma stood behind me and dropped a black stone necklace around my neck, making me dip down so she could fasten it for me. She did her ritual pulling up of the dress so my cleavage wasn't showing and smiled at me. I had not felt so happy in such a long time.

I walked down the stairs feeling very much the princess. My mum and dad stood staring at me, one of them burst into tears and I can tell you it was not the woman of the pair. I stood in the middle of the living room letting their eyes gaze at me and only felt the tinniest bit of discomfort. My other feelings were no doubt, pride, happiness and vanity. My friends started turning up and we were all crying and admiring each other. The girls looked beautiful and the boys looked so incredibly handsome. The limo arrived and we set off for an hour drive of luxury.

We soon arrived at school and everyone began smiling and taking pictures. I felt like a famous person. A red carpet had been set out on the ground and we were ushered across it into the lecture theatre. I remember this as one of the best memories because as I walked through the hallway the ex-friend, who had hounded me for my entire last year of school, looked round to us late comers. Her face dropped and her expression spoke louder than words. That face spoke pure jealousy and envy. I smiled at her in the loveliest way possible. Stare all you want bitch I'm so much more fortunate than you will ever be.

We were told all about good behaviour and not to have too much fun and we were soon on our way to the prom location. The whole night I danced with friends, danced with the cute boys, danced with drunken teachers. Half way through, I was told very quickly that I had to make a speech to thank Mrs Roache and I had to do it in five minutes. Thanks for the heads up guys.

I got head boy and the other prefects together and stood by the DJ asking if we could make a speech. The microphone was given to me and I was expected to do all the talking. Thanks again guys! The ex-friend stood in the audience sulking as she was not included, and we all had a cry and a cheer for the teachers and what they had done for us.

The night was truly amazing. My family I cannot thank enough for making it so beautiful, and if some divine intervention had helped make this night perfect for me then I have to thank them a million times over. Your kindness has not been forgotten.

15

I remember one night mum and I had a huge argument. I can't tell you for the life of me what it was about, but it was serious enough to have us both angry and upset. I must tell you that my mum and I never argue, so if we ever do, it must be serious.

We said the most horrible things to each other and in the end I stormed up the stairs crying. I got on my laptop and on MSN. Everywhere on peoples statuses I saw messages, 'Sorry for your loss Tom.' 'All my love to Tom and family.' I asked a friend what was going on.

"Tom from our year, his mum just died."

I went numb with shock. His mum had gone to sleep that night and never woke up. Simple as that. My mind began to work overtime wondering how and why. Had they made plans for a day that would never arrive? What were her last words to her son, my friend Tom?

My poor friend Tom. What could he possibly be feeling right now? I couldn't bear to imagine. The horror and pain of his situation made me think of my own mum, and what I had just said to her. The thought of losing her made me feel sick. Devastation so strong overcame me and I fell to the floor crying. I cried from guilt, I cried from overwhelming love for my mum, and I cried for Tom.

Mum walked upstairs to my room with some mystic intuition and saw me there on the floor. She fell down next to me and I held her so tightly, crying onto her shoulder. Through sobbing gasps I told her about Tom's mum. I told her how much I love her and how I never want to lose her.

"I'm sorry mummy, I'm sorry,"

We spent the next hour crying for Tom and his family. Since that night, my mum and I have never been closer.

16

I got ready, so carefully and deliberately, not wanting to put the last piece of clothing on that would confirm I was ready to go downstairs. I was scared. Beyond scared, panic was gnawing at my insides in a sickening grasp. I tried to think back about the exams I may have done well in. Drama was a part of me, so I couldn't have done too badly there. Construction, I loved construction more than I expected I would. I had done my work experience on a construction site. There had been so many good times spent with the lads, two other girls and Mr Gildea, chucking mortar at each other and blaming the start of the fight on the opposite sex.

What else had I been good at? That was it. Science, Mr Orrell, Mr Hewitt and Mr Fisher had been very patient with me and I enjoyed the lessons, but I wasn't very good at them. English no idea. Maths . . . gosh I'm crap at maths, always have been. I was going to fail, no doubt about it. The depression hadn't helped how could I possibly pass? Well I wasn't, clearly.

I wrote down what I could do in the event that I failed. I could carry on acting; you don't need Pythagoras theorem when performing a monologue on stage. I could try and work with my dad. He could forget the fact that I had ruined my future and hire me. My dad, my family, they are going to be so disappointed. They will hate me; I can't have them hate me. I could run away . . . No don't be so stupid, I won't do that bad. Will I?

I walked round the corner to my school, living close had its uses. I signed in and walked into the lunch hall where the results were being kept. I went to the desk with my surname initial and picked up my envelope.

"Are you going to open that now Annabella?" My head teacher Mr Roberts asked, rather too loudly that people near inched closer to hear.

"No I promised to tell my family first sir."

"Well, go have a picture taken with you smiling I'm sure you've done well." He must know the results. Maybe that was a sign that I hadn't done too badly.

I walked to my construction teacher who was carrying a pile of papers rolled up in his hand.

"You've done well Annabella don't worry." Well maybe this is good, I haven't failed I've done okay. I shook his hand and ran back home, nearly triggering an asthma attack in the process.

I sat on the sofa and found my dad's number in my contacts. I pressed the green button and it automatically dialled.

"Hello"

"Hey dad it's me, I've got them here."

"Right ok open them, I'll stay on the line here." I put the phone on the sofa next to me and opened the envelope. The words going round in my head went something like the F word with a load of prayers with it. I took the papers out, putting the phone back to my ear.

"Okay, science C, drama A, art C, construction AB, maths . . ."

"What!?"

"C! English language B, English literature A, history C, all science C."

We both burst into tears. Three A's, two B's and five C's. I know they weren't all A*, but for someone like me who struggled with these lessons, especially maths, I was expected D's. I had hoped to get all C's. So the A's and B's included made me feel magnificent.

My dad was so proud of me, which matters the most because I was and am always trying to make him proud. I instantly felt hope in the fact that if in the event I wanted to change the world with a paragraph in a newspaper or build a wall to stop a natural disaster, I could do these quite easily and my GCSE paper could substantiate that.

I was very happy and failure was no longer the option. I had succeeded in my own standards set out before me, and I had made myself proud which is an often overlooked skill. I must again thank the teachers at Castlebrook High for their help and support. If it was just a miracle, then I again thank the divine intervention that swapped my papers with some smart person.

My brother and sister gave me a card; they must have had two, one saying congratulations and another saying keep strong. I phoned my mum at work and she began crying and telling random customers the news.

I was going off to college to study performing arts. I had created a banner saying 'Piss off" to the people who had hurt me so badly. I was feeling euphoric all of a sudden and I felt pride in my own abilities. As Richard Bach said, *'Ask yourself the secret of YOUR success. Listen to your answer, and practice it.'*

17

Going into college felt like a new start. I was leaving some dark times behind and leaving the people responsible for them. For the next two years I was going to be studying just performing arts. This to me really is my kind of heaven.

There were three groups, Acting, Dancing and Musical Theatre. I was in musical theatre as I figured I might as well learn all three, if in the event I do end up on the west end, which wouldn't be a bad thing. So that's what I did. For two years I acted, I danced and I sang.

We had great acting tutors James, Dave and Lisa. Lisa is an incredibly pretty woman, who always encouraged us to not care what we looked like on stage, just as long as we were performing right. I remember thinking it was easy for her as she could pull the most stupid faces imaginable and still look beautiful.

James is very intelligent and would impress us with his conversations complete with every word from the dictionary. I think we all improved our acting techniques by pretending we understood what he said.

Dave is very funny and loved to put us through meditation techniques. In his classes we were bent into all types of shapes, and if we managed them we were instantly gymnasts and could compete in the Olympics.

Our head of year Andy was wonderful. He was such a great tutor to look up too. We could talk about anything and he would be not only a teacher, he was also a friend.

Singing teachers were rare as there were a lot of mix ups with singing staff at the time, however there was on teacher we called Debs who would always give me a cuddle when I needed one.

The scariest and most brilliant teacher however was our dance teacher, Jools. I'm 5"4 on a good day; she must have only reached to my chest area. But with her bright red hair and energy to match a six year old overdosing on milkyways and red bull, you could always tell when she was in the vicinity. At times she was the scariest woman in the world. But when you got through to the soft, gushy side she kept hidden, she was secretly a truly lovely and beautiful woman.

Every day was different, every day was unique. I guess that is the beauty about the performing world. No job would be the same, no character is the same. I had made friends and for a while I could be myself, and not need to worry about the depression.

I could stand up and start dancing and no one would take a second glance. In fact most would stand up and join me. Every day felt wonderful and strange. Every day we would laugh. It is such a relief to be able to laugh and feel completely free of feeling like the strange, odd one out.

One day I had brought in a book, the wonderful author, Lisa Kleypas, writes such wonderful historical romances. I can escape easily in her books because I fit in more with the different era, and the men are just gorgeous. Anyway, these books describe some romantic scenes, which really just lead on to more erotic scenes. As I was reading one of these books my friends grabbed the book from my hands and ran off with it. They teased me a little with these books because whenever I read a particularly . . . sexual scene, I would blush, and then they knew I was reading one of the more passionate scenes. My friends ran off taking the book to our tutor James and I had to stand there with the others whilst James read aloud a random paragraph in the book, *"Fumbling at the fastenings of his platoons, he freed himself and climbed over her, and pushed her thighs wide. Slowly he nudged against her and pressed inside. She cried out, helplessly tightening against his entry, but it was too late; he had already sunk deep into the clinging heat of her body."*

It was certainly an experience hearing him read out these sentences, everyone else stood there enjoying my humiliation, I cursed them all as I listened to James utter the last sentence. I grabbed the book from his hands and he looked at me with a kind of judgemental knowledge, that this description would probably excite me if it was happening in real life. I took a walk of shame back down the corridor with my friends grouped around me hugging me and telling me they accept my sexually frustrated self. Yes thank you guys, thanks for the understanding.

18

"She killed herself. She killed herself because of us."

I walk on hearing the friends crying.

"No, it's because of you she is dead!"

I look around at the angry face of the friend before me, and the confused and sad faces of the others.

"I didn't do anything." I whisper.

"Of course you did, you had to make her feel like shit, you just had to get so high and fucking mighty. You pushed her buttons and now she's dead!"

"Please, I, I didn't mean to argue with her, I didn't mean to say what I said, I, please."

"No! You are a disgusting person and because of you she is dead!" My friends leave me to cry my guilt to the air. I walk slowly to the chair and sob even more.

Suddenly my friend Adam is there, walking towards me. He sits beside me, "It wasn't your fault you know."

"Adam it was. I pushed her buttons and if I had been nice if I had been more patient, this would never have happened. She would still be here."

"She had to be told someday, but the answer wasn't suicide. It was all just bad timing. She needed help but, there was no way we could have helped her. She should have found another answer."

"I will pretend to believe you, but I can't say that I do."

"Then I will just have to spend the rest of my life telling you until you do."

I smile at him. (Though I do not believe him, my heart has lightened a little.) "What have you got in your hand?"

"Nothing," he replies.

"Tell me please."

"It's just something I was writing."

"It's one of your songs isn't it?" He remains silent but looks away in defeat.

"Please let me see Adam."

"No."

"Sing it to me."

"No."

"Then I will just go to the police now and say it's my fault a friend is dead."

"Don't start that! Fine."

I smile with success and begin to listen to the voice, his voice. He sings of love, singing such beautiful words.

He stops and we sit in silence for a minute, letting the echo of his voice fade away.

"That was beautiful Adam."

"I wrote it for you."

"Oh Adam, why is life so . . ." He holds my chin and stares into my eyes.

"It is horrible and cruel, but not all of it has to be, it doesn't have to be with us anyway."

"You can't promise such a thing." I whisper.

"No, but I can bloody well try with you." He holds me and we kiss. So softly, so sweetly, I hold on to him and we kiss some more.

Suddenly we stop and turn to the audience. The rest of our drama class are sat watching us. They are so silent, just staring at us. Me and Adam shift awkwardly. I smile at my best friends, Angie and Rachel, hoping to get some reaction. Suddenly one person begins to clap, and then the rest follow. We both sag in relief. Maybe we didn't do too badly after all.

My friend and I blush slightly trying to erase the cringing memories of what felt like a taboo kiss between brother and sister. We soon forget though. We got great comments from our teacher Carol Godbey, and we did a good performance, which was all that mattered.

When the lesson has ended Angie and I were told to stay behind. We had both auditioned for a play the theatre group was doing, and we both got main parts! It is very rare I can have a full brilliant day, but I was having such a good time now, I think I went to sleep smiling.

19

You can't reason yourself into cheerfulness any more than you can reason yourself into an extra six inches in height.—Stephen Fry.

I was having some form of breakdown. My breathing was laboured and I knew I needed to get out. I didn't care where just out. I ran through the door when everyone was working and threw myself into the bathroom. I held myself in the cubicle, hoping to still my shaking body, and burst into tears. Jools later came in and found me. She took me to an empty classroom and made me talk to her. I told her what I felt and the reasons behind it, the bullying, the depression, the complete lack of self-control as my mind broke down gradually.

She gave me a big hug and told me things would be alright and that she would help in any way she could. She told me to get my bags from the room and to go home early, to give myself some space and time to recover. I felt so much better after she had found me.

As some of you may know, depression doesn't always just go away. A line I would hear a lot would be, 'Pull yourself out of it'. Not an easy thing to do and only people with depression will understand how something as pulling yourself together, can be the most impossible thing to do in the world. Now that someone knew about what was going on sent a huge relief through my mind.

The tutors now understood that if I ever acted erratically or needed to get out I had a reason for doing so. I couldn't thank the tutors enough for helping me through it. There were some times the depression really got the better of me however. For any production we did we would all have to audition, just as normal actors would. I remember for the last musical I had been suffering so badly with it. I couldn't concentrate on the monologue I had to learn and the song I had to sing got the better of me. I went into the studio at my allotted audition time and began my monologue. I could not finish the third line, no matter how many times I attempted it I just couldn't finish. Jools told me to move on to my song and I couldn't even start it. I ran out of the room and back into that bathroom cubicle. I failed myself in that room. I had let the depression take over me. I had let it invade my mind, as easily as you could rip a piece of paper. I had let it take control of me, and now I was facing that consequence. If I let this happen every time I had an audition I would never get any work, or anywhere with my life. It was a good time to get hit with a bucket of water. The realisation was like an electric shock, that for the first time, the only thing stopping me getting what I wanted was me.

Another example of this came when I was asked to play the wicked witch of the west in the second year panto of The Wizard of Oz. We were going up to Edinburgh to perform it at the fringe festival. An obviously great opportunity for a first year in college.

I had told my family to take the ritual trip to Scotland for two weeks, whilst I stayed at home. The thought of being with people, even people I loved felt impossible. I wanted to be alone. I felt myself turning into a cold, lonely . . . monster. I needed my family to get away from me and I needed to be away from everyone else.

I lay on the sofa a lot, hating who I was, what I had become. Not wanting to eat, sleep, or even shower. Every day feeling the same. So many times grandma wanted me to stay with her, but I couldn't. I couldn't see anyone. She desperately wanted to stay with me, but she could not leave grandad by himself. She phoned me every few hours and I knew each time I told her I was okay; she would put down the phone and cry. I loved her so much, but I couldn't stand the questions, I couldn't stand the fuss.

Through this time I was asked to go to Edinburgh but I told my teacher, Barbara, that I couldn't. She tried to find a way around my predicament but she couldn't convince me to go. She said I should see a doctor and try and get myself sorted. The scariest phone call I've ever endured was trying to see a doctor.

My best friend Lauren arrived at my doorstep to stay over one night and keep me company. I put Pride and Prejudice on with Keira Knightly and Matthew McFadden. Lauren was really the only friend who stuck by me through the last year of school, I couldn't thank her enough.

When my parents got home, my grandma told them that they needed to speak to me immediately. I had to tell them why I wasn't myself. I explained how I had felt for now two years. It was so incredibly difficult; I would rather have gone through a minefield or jumped from a plane.

I had now addressed these problems and needed help urgently. I couldn't let it take over me as it had done so many times before. I couldn't waste any more opportunities.

By the end of the year it seemed to disappear for a while. Which was good as it was just in time for panto. Barbara was directing the panto and I was terrified she would not give me a role because of how I had left her in the lurch with Edinburgh. My audition went well and on the day we were told our roles she asked me if I was strong enough to do this. I begged her to give me the role I deserved and that I was fine now. I hoped so desperately that I wasn't about to drag myself down again. We all waited in the lunch hall for the cast list to be put up. So many of us pretended we didn't care what we got but secretly hoped for the good parts. Someone ran in saying the cast list was up and a whole mass of performance students rushed out into the corridor towards the notice board.

I saw my name on the piece of paper and smiled. We were doing the panto Aladdin, and I was Sultana. As in the Sultans latest gold digging wife. I was incredibly happy and phoned my parents immediately.

Panto was the most fun I had ever had. We were constantly laughing and joking. I borrowed clothes from my friend Fareena. Our Arabian set was up and we all looked beautiful in our beautiful, vibrant costumes.

The children came in through the day and were supplied with drinks and ice lollies. Every actor must feel that same euphoria when performing on stage. The lights bearing down on you, showing your ever facial feature and movement. Your energy bouncing off your fellow actors on stage. Intensifying that feeling of happiness and excitement. That first slice of adrenaline still coursing through your body, lighting up your face and burning your blood like fire, working your heart faster, your excitement buzzing in your ears till you struggle to hear.

I stood at the wings waiting for my cue line to be spoken to make my grand entrance. I walked on stage, all bold and regal, my voice vibrating of the walls, my energy high and intense. I went to the first row of the audience and began my audience bating and soon became the dame, having the audience 'boo' and giggle. I was experiencing the feelings of power, having an audience in my grasp. Controlling them with my voice, my movements.

All eyes on you as you work your way round the stage. There can't be a more surreal feeling in the world. Allowing this magic to take hold of you, working its way into the world around you. There are people who think acting is useless and told me so regularly, but we live in a world of performing and spectating, and I can guarantee you do both on a daily basis.

But acting is now in my blood. I sold my soul to drama the moment I stepped into my first acting class. The feeling I get of pure happiness and delight. The drunk/drugged feeling when performing on stage. Blood racing, heart pounding. Coming back to life, being able to escape all the shit that is going on in your world. Taking on a new role, a new character, telling a story, your story, anybody's story and seeing the audience clap their hands and shout in applause at the wonderful thing you just did.

So many of us every day will watch a film, or go to a theatre. Listen to music or see a concert. All to escape the dark times in life and find a new happier world. Whether it is to see a play or listen to a song each one amounts to the same thing. It allows you to connect, keep you company with the knowledge that you are not alone. Let your mind wander to a time you can be happy. To a time where that darkness was just a distant memory.

We had more performances like this, some more serious than panto. We did a piece on 'Time' which included voice recordings from the victims of 9/11, calling their loved ones to say goodbye for the last time. Hearing some of them left a fair few of us crying on the spot. James being our director had a lot of deep ideas that could be used which took us weeks to understand. Some ideas we performed I am still trying to work out.

Another piece we did was about a woman called Sarah Kane who had dealt with a lot of mental health issues. The particular piece we worked on was an actual diary extract she kept whilst living in a mental hospital. It was definitely a mind mess up for anyone reading it. I felt so comfortable with this kind of play I feared for my own sanity. I could relate to what she felt. This made me even more fearful. Was this going to be me one day?

In college I began going out more and enjoying myself. But there were also the times my depression got the better of me and I couldn't bear to leave the safety of my home. For this I lost friends, something I deeply regret.

Parties are always good for performance students considering we don't need alcohol to have fun. We are always complete nutters which make us quite easy to get along with strangely enough.

We are also known for being a horny lot too! Don't worry we don't experiment with group orgies in class. We are just very passionate and excitable; which in turn makes us more cheeky and confident. One time I was used as a human rubber doll and bent into different sex poses and told which was better for the man or the woman. In all fairness you learnt a lot.

So many times Jools would make us walk down the length of the dance studio to some form of Cabaret music and make us perform our best showgirl impressions. Strangely enough I never had a problem portraying the prostitute parts. In fact it was pointed out that I was the most believable . . . Charming!

For a Christmas present I had my name changed to incorporate my Scottish heritage. But paperwork is always five years behind so I didn't exist in college for part of the time. Fortunately because of this I was put into the new performing arts course that was due to start the year after I left. This course meant that you could achieve distinction * if your grades were higher. As I was the only one on this new course in my year I was then the only one who achieved triple distinction * when I finished college. I was incredibly proud but I got it completely by accident. Tip-change your name sometime and spice up the system! You may get awarded for it.

College had become a mass of performing, costumes and laughter. I had performed in some wonderful plays. Danced till I collapsed on the living room rug when I got home. Applied so much make-up and changed into so many different costumes. Even in the most stressful parts of college there was always someone laughing and joking to lighten the mood, even if it was to laugh at all our discomforts. Tutors were friends who were always there to help. For the first time, I felt truly at home in a place I belonged. It was a safe haven where we crazy stage performers could be ourselves. In a world where we are constantly told to grow up and stop dreaming. To live in the real world. Instead we just lived in our own version of the real world.

". . . and there I suddenly found my articulate self in a dazzling land of smiling, jostling people wearing and not wearing all sorts of costumes and doing all sorts of clever things. And that's when I knew! What other life could there be but that of an actor?"
—Cary Grant

20

We are going to the Lake District today. I am so excited! I hope we see Beatrix Potter's house. She is one of my idols, to think she had done something so rare for her gender. Become this successful, rich woman working in a man's world. Doing what she loved. Making people happy. Her heartbreak when her fiancé, Norman Wayne died. Her fight back to save the land she loved. She is a true inspiration, and I'm going to the source.

It is so beautiful. The sun has revealed himself so bright and hot. Everyone looks happy. How could they not be in such a beautiful place! We walked into a little shop that sells Beatrix Potter memorabilia. I bought a key ring of Jemima Puddle duck, and a book on Beatrix's life and stories.

We climb aboard a ferry, and sit on the top deck, taking us across to Ambleside. There are houses on the other side of the lake, which must belong to rich people because they are huge! As we get nearer we see a little harbour with lots of little wooden boats tied up. A small village near the water appears. I can see some shops and a pub surrounded by trees. People are crowding everywhere.

We step ashore and make our way through the crowds. We find a seat at the busy pub right next to the lake. The water is a deep shade of blue, the current causes the boats to tap gently against each other. The sun is glistening like diamonds on to the water. I can see the reflections of the hillside across the lake. It is that calm and clear. All the colours are extremely vibrant. Bright yellows, greens and blues. All intoxicating colours making you catch your breath when you stare too long. No wonder Beatrix felt inspired here. It's the kind of place that lets your spirit soar. Taking your imagination to places it cannot easily hide from. I have to go back, I need too. We were on the wrong side of the lake from her house but we will go back again and see it. I can hardly wait!

21

Can I make you jealous? Well I am going to anyway. Although if you're not a Harry Potter fan you probably won't care.

I went to the world premiere for the last Harry Potter film! I was there by accident really. Dad knew a man who had tickets. They were for him and his father, but the father had been taken ill and gave his ticket to my dad. But there was some hesitation about whether the son would be going or not. It turned out that he wasn't so he gave the extra ticket to my dad. So being the biggest fan in my family I was going with him!

We arrived in London and checked in at the Hilton Hotel in Hyde Park. Dad dressed very handsomely in a suit and I dressed in a beautiful little black dress with red shoes and a red clutch bag. We took the tube to Trafalgar Square and I have never felt more boxed up in my life. In fact I think I know how sardines feel.

We walked out and decided to follow another couple who were dressed up like royalty, hoping they were dressed up for the same reason. Thankfully they were and were leading us right to the premiere.

Some guards checked our tickets and we were lead on to the red carpet. The actual red carpet! Rows upon rows of cameramen were stood at the sides in front of a sign with the country they were reporting from. Japan,

Germany, Australia, America, all there filming us walk past!

I tried to walk as quickly as possible as people were cheering me not realising I wasn't famous at all. I didn't want to disappoint. But it is hard to rush when you are walking on clouds. Your dreams unravelling in front of you.

It was the longest red carpet put out at a premiere so we had a long way to go. The areas of the carpet that were not visible to the crowds had parts of the Harry Potter set on it. The banners of the different houses were hung up, Ravenclaw, Gryffindor, Hufflepuff and Slytherin. Olivanders wand shop was there surrounded by cauldron's and other props. A stretch table had been laid out holding three beautiful owls, a white owl, like Hedwig, stood in the middle.

As we progressed further on the carpet a group of death eaters were stood nearby. I asked dad to take a picture of me with them. Obviously they were not real death eaters, I still felt slightly nervous nearing them. I stood a few paces away keeping my distance and faced the camera for my dad to take the picture. All of a sudden the group ran up behind me frightening me half to death. My dad laughed at me nearly wetting myself but I managed to relax. They stood with me posing whilst he took the picture and I very nervously thanked them.

Finally we neared the end of the carpet, and walked into the cinema. The film was incredible, is incredible. I tried not to cry but it was difficult not too. The first Harry Potter film came out in 2001. I was eight years old. The last film being released in 2011. Ten years Harry Potter had been a part of my life, and always will be. It became an era where my childhood was ending. I was growing up. Just as the characters were growing up also. The books had been the only thing I wanted and the lessons JK Rowling had taught us have stayed in my mind all this time. I had a place I could escape too. It was almost as if I could believe a magical place existed. A place so much better than the 'muggle' world I lived in.

After the film, we got on to the coaches and were taken away to the after party location. The entrance was surrounded by photographers and reporters trying to force their way in. A very big and rather scary looking bouncer checked our tickets and let us through. The excitement was breaking through me. All my idols were crammed together in this very room and I was about to meet them.

We looked around the room and I turned towards my dad, my eyes widened like saucers as I recognised a face standing further behind him. It was Helena Bonham-Carter! I couldn't believe it! I was giddy with hysterics and my dad nearly was also.

I decided to start my autograph spree. I went to Helena first. I left dad holding the camera and my bag and nervously walked towards her. The distance shortened rapidly, I was only a couple paces from her. This woman is such an inspiration to me and I was about to meet her. I waited for a child to get his autograph and then it was my turn.

She looked stunned for a moment and focused her eyes on my black diamond necklace my grandma had bought me for prom and said, "Is that my . . . no it can't be . . . What's your name?" I shook my head and looked down at my chest and back up at her. "Annabella". She signed her name and gave me the piece of paper back. I thanked her and then walked back to my dad.

Still on a high from meeting Helena Bonham-Carter I saw Alan Rickman! I walked up to him and waited for a little girl to get his autograph. She turned to me and asked if I was an actress. To which I replied, "One day I hope I will be." She smiled at me and walked off, feeling rather happy I moved my gaze up to Alan's. He stared at me in such a Snape manner I immediately thought, 'ten seconds with Alan Rickman and I've already pissed him off'.

I asked if I could get his autograph, he signed his name and gave me back the piece of paper. I thanked him and ran back to dad. I had just met another true inspiration. The high was not going to go away easily.

Soon I had met Julie Walters, another idol. Matthew Lewis, Mark Williams, Rupert Grint and Danny from Mcfly. I was even a foot away from JK Rowling. By the time I got to her though she was ushered away by her guards. I had been so bloody close to meeting her!

I have to say though, the best people I could meet that night, had to be Tom Felton and Jonathan Ross. I had been waiting round the other actors, asking for their autographs and getting pushed back by their bodyguards. So I was rather exhausted when I got to Tom. However I was completely shocked by how gorgeous he was, yes in looks but how he was with his fans. He was taking time out to talk to them, get his picture taken with the children. Being a completely lovely celebrity to his fans when I had been chasing the other actors around like a vulture and being cut off like a headless chicken.

It got to my turn and he asked how I was enjoying myself and wrote his name on my piece of paper. He then winked and smiled at me and I immediately became a pool at his feet.

The next amazing guy I met was the wonderful Jonathan Ross. My dad spotted him whilst I was stuffing my face with the food at the buffet and pushed me along to his table. I walked slowly towards him and was about to apologise for disturbing him when suddenly he stood up and reached his hand out to shake mine. I was in so much shock that he would immediately treat me like a normal human being I nearly dropped the items I was carrying. I shook his hand and he signed his name on my piece of paper. I couldn't get over how kind he was; such a little gesture meant so much to me. I was being treated like an equal to someone who was a star in my eyes.

They had the biggest chocolate fountain with so many desserts to dip in. A hog roast was cooking outside on the patio and a table stood near covered with all kinds of treats to go with it.

One day, a normal girl went to a film premiere, and met her idols. Her devotion to these films had taken up half her life. But now it was time to say goodbye. She had stuck with Harry . . . until the very end.

22

It was Christmas Day. We had received beautiful presents and had a wonderful dinner. It got later into the night and I went upstairs to my room to get a book. Suddenly I heard a scream. I ran down the stairs moving so quickly I almost fell, and ran into the living room where my family were. I saw my dad on the sofa looking dazed and confused. My mum and sister were standing in front of him, holding each other and crying. I asked what had happened, but no one spoke. I shouted again angrily, asking what had just happened. My sister, in broken gasps, told me that dad had been coughing and had dropped his head and stopped breathing. They had believed he had died there and then.

We called an ambulance and I watched my daddy being taken away. His heart was beating three hundred times a minute. Some of the nurses had said they had never seen a heartbeat that quick. They told my mum that the only thing they could do to slow it down, would be to stop the heart completely.

There was a chance however that they would not be able to start it up again. They stopped his heart, took the defibrillator and pumped the electric into his chest.

His heart was beating. He was going to be okay. My daddy was going to be okay.

23

My mums beautiful friends Geraldine (very Irish) and Derek (very Scottish) were getting married. We flew over to Malta where the wedding was to take place.

It wasn't the warmest time to go. If it wasn't raining it was windy as hell. But I took every opportunity to explore. The place was teeming with nuns, so wherever I walked I took good care to wear suitable clothing just in case.

The ceremony was beautiful, and even I cried which was a shock when what I really felt for them was fear and the choking grip of commitment! When the deed was done Derek raised his arm in a champion lift and we all walked into the main room for the speeches and food.

When it was time to leave, I had the difficult task of driving my drunken parents back to the apartment. Not an easy thing when they are the only ones who know the way back and are slurring their words!

Dad took us to the film set where Popeye was filmed. The 1980 film starring Robin Williams and Shelley Duvall. It was brilliant seeing the film set where Robin had once stepped. However it was a shame that it was now being used as an amusement park, with a tacky song and dance show every so often, and most of the buildings closed down. However I can't say no to a visit to a film set. After all, they are a perfect dreamland to me.

Near our apartment stood a beautiful church which held a vast marble dome on top. At night the dome would light up, making it the brightest spectacle in the vicinity. Bells would chime every hour declaring the time to the town. I found the sound so enchanting I would stand on the balcony and just listen to each toll sound.

Eventually I decided to walk up to the church. A statue of a saint stood in the middle of an exquisite little courtyard, reaching his hand out to curious souls. Trees surrounded the walls that crumbled with age, adding a charming quality to the place.

I walked in and found people praying. Trying not to disturb, I crept away from the congregation and went through the back hallways to see what I could find. I saw a glass shelf which held the skull of what I can assume was an old saint or priest.

Across the walls held relics of the church's history. The deeper I went into the hallway the darker it became. The passage was lit by candles and I had to squint to see what was on the walls. I could see letters, thousands of letters. With some of the letters I saw, crutches, bandages, casts for leg or arm or head injuries. I tried to read some of the letters but most of them were written in foreign languages. Some however I did find in English. A woman wrote of how her son has been injured and according to doctors he would be unable to walk for the rest of his life. But when all their hope had been lost, the son had miraculously learnt to stand up and walk again.

According to these people, they were lost causes. They had given up hope, and all of a sudden their prayers had been answered. Miracles had been performed, and the only person they could thank, was God. I did not know if this was a real divine intervention. Sometimes we can shock ourselves into performing our own miracles. Sometimes doctors can find the cures. Or maybe it really could be a miracle. A cure from God who had answered these peoples prayers. I did not know what the answer was. But I didn't mind. Around me I could see the hope and gratitude of individuals who had given up on both. Their prayers, their hopes had been answered. Now they were happy, and thankful for what they had been given. I could not help but feel moved, in this passage of miracles, in this darkened hall of hope.

24

Ffyona walked down the stairs, looking as beautiful as ever. She was wearing a red, fish tail dress with diamante beading across the top. Her hair swept over her shoulder in a beautiful mass of black, silk curls. Mum, gran and I were all in tears. I was so proud of my little sister, so proud of the beautiful, young lady she had turned into.

Fe, as I call her, is my best friend. I have watched her grow from my cute, baby sister, to this. Sweet, funny, kind to everyone she meets. She is my best friend, my soul mate. I am the luckiest sister in the world to have her. She makes us laugh with her innocent principles of life. She can be feather brained sometimes. In an actual GCSE cooking exam she was asked what the V stood for on packaging. Obviously it is vegetarian but Fairy Fe forgot what exam she was in and answered 'a roman numeral for five.' This is right I guess but as this was a cooking exam, the answer should have announced itself in her brain.

Her friends soon arrived and all were looking very gorgeous. Grandma had not been feeling well for a long time but she kept a smile on her face and complimented each of my sister's friends, telling them how wonderful they all looked. I loved the lads in their suits. I find it so nice seeing boys actually look like men for a change.

The group got into the limo and were soon on their way. We promised to meet her at school so we could see her off again. Grandma was feeling so ill though, she is one to carry on through her pain as if nothing is wrong, but it must have been bad that she needed to leave. She so hated not to be able to see Ffyona at school, but she couldn't pretend anymore.

My beautiful grandma. She has white fluffy hair, which inspired me to nickname her cotton bud. Speaking in a strong Scottish dialect other people struggle to understand her, but I do not. I was brought up with her voice and can understand her perfectly well. She is incredibly kind, and beautiful. She would do absolutely anything for anyone. Grandma helped raise us. With dad having to work a lot we really had mum and grandma. Two beautiful, strong women to live up too.

I can't tell you reader how much I love her. We have a little secret kiss. One of us will put our eyelashes gently on the other and blink rapidly, tickling the other one. We call it a butterfly kiss and she laughs with her little titter every time we do.

When I was still small enough to fit into a shopping trolley she would often enjoy annoying mum, using me as bate. I would ask for things to eat as we were walking through the store (mostly Peperami-I would eat the whole packet before we got to the check-out.) When mum said no, grandma would tell me to call mum something. In the middle of ASDA I would shout out "BITCH" to my own mum. She would turn around and stare at me with the scariest eyes only a mum can give. My grandma would be tittering behind.

I drove her back home and tucked her up in bed.

"You sure you'll be alright?"

"Yes, I will be fine, don't worry about me go see Fefe off."

"Okay." I bent down and gave her a kiss. She looked so sad and ill. I felt I should have stayed with her, but I knew she would have been more upset if I missed my sister leaving from school.

A couple hours later me and 'the mothers' were sat in the garden, drinking and talking. My dad was upset that he had not been able to see her as he had needed to work. Other than that however the night had been perfect. My sister had her special night and we were so happy and proud of her. Little did I know however, that these were going to be some of the last wonderful days, before our lives changed forever.

25

I walk into the Lloyds TSB bank with grandma. She wants to sort something out; I'm just here to spend some time with her. The line is taking forever, but we can keep each other amused easily.

"I'm not feeling very well." She tells me. She looks round to see where the nearest chairs are.

"Do you want to go and sit down for a bit?"

"No." She insists, "I'm fine." She just wants to complete her errand.

Suddenly she grips my arms and I hold her so tightly, scared of this sudden incident unfolding. Within seconds she is falling. It seems she is falling so slowly, when in fact it only takes a few short seconds. I try so hard to keep her from tumbling, but she has become a dead weight and unbelievably heavy for someone so small.

She bangs her head against the floor. I hear the sound of the impact. She has completely collapsed and almost brought me down with her. I scream and cry for her to wake up. I see people running past me but their faces are shadows, their voices fading into the distance. I manage to hear someone say phone an ambulance and even though he may not have directed it to me I could think of nothing else to do. I pick up my phone and dial 999. I am asked for the police or ambulance services and I cry out ambulance. I am soon passed on to a woman who asks me to explain what was happening. I try to keep as calm as possible but it is difficult. I am so incredibly scared.

What am I to do? What is wrong with my beautiful, wonderful grandma? I am told that an ambulance would arrive shortly and I put the phone down.

At this point my grandma is starting to come round. A lovely woman from the bank is kneeling on the other side of my grandma looking after us both. We are applying wet cloths to her head and making sure her breathing is regular. My grandma looks ashamed and guilty at having these people make a fuss over her. That was just my grandma, feeling bad for others taking the time out to help her.

I phone my dad and he follows us in the ambulance. I have spent so much time riding in the back of an ambulance at the moment I could tell you very well in detail what each corner of one looks like.

They do not know what is wrong, but they have to stitch up the part of her head that had made contact with the floor, the part I had been unable to protect.

26

"Dad, there is like an agency thing on Facebook and there are some auditions for a new dance film called Believe."

"Oh right?"

"Yeah, well the nearest one to us is in Blackpool and it's in two weeks, so can I please, please go?"

"Why are you asking me?"

"Well I kind of need someone to take me."

"I thought there was a reason, of course I'll take you."

We are near Blackpool now. I remember coming here with gran when I was a little girl. We got asked to go on a radio station. I was asked how many bulbs it took to light up the Blackpool tower. I was given two answers and had to pick one. I guessed any because I didn't have a clue but it was the right one! I got some goodies and we later got to hear the interview on the radio. It was such a lovely day.

We park up at the centre and dad looks at my face which is turning whiter by the second. "Just try your best, that's all you can to do." I get a sticker with a number on and wait. We wait for hours sat at a table looking over the garden. This is the worst part, the waiting. I would like to just walk in do my audition and walk back out again.

Not thinking about how scared I was or how I could have done better.

We are put into groups and are taught a dance routine by the director Michael. The routine is very street dance and I suddenly find myself in one of them, 'What the hell were you thinking' moments. Strangely however I manage to keep up. I jump up from my knees without falling backwards and somehow keep up with the other dancers. I keep in time with the music and incredibly I seem to be doing it right. Michael turns off the music and the judges write down something on their individual pieces of paper.

They are writing down the good ones aren't they? Michael explains that they didn't bring the camera they had packed to film us and apologised for their forgetfulness. I decide that they are just humouring us and have already chosen people, so I leave the room with a heavy heart.

When the day ends dad and I get ready to go home. I take one last look at the beach and the shops surrounding the amusement park. My heart feels even heavier.

"I'm sorry dad."

"For what?"

"Making you waste your day off for me."

"Don't be silly, you haven't wasted it at all."

Months I have heard nothing, even though I know what the answer will be. I decide to check my e-mails anyway. Wait, I see one. From Michael, he has sent me an e-mail! Oh gosh wait, what if it's a rejection one? 'Sorry but you aren't good enough for this film.'

I open the e-mail and wait for it too load, oh gosh hurry up.

'Thank you for your interest in and recent audition for our forthcoming film "Believe".

After seeing thousands of people at auditions across the United Kingdom, and receiving as many clips from many talented performers across the world, I would like to congratulate you, as you have been selected as a cast member for the film!
We are offering you to role of:

Dancer—*this will include performance in any of the dance scenes included in the film. If a main role becomes vacant, I will look upon everyone in an acting, singing or dancing role to find a suitable person before advertising elsewhere.*'

I have a part! Even a little part in an actual film! I can't believe it! I run upstairs screaming to everyone. Mum reads it and then dad. Both are crying and laughing. I go to Jon and Fe and they are laughing also. We are all so happy! I phone grandma and tell her the news. She is ecstatic. I can hear her trying to tell grandad. I drive down to see her and she hugs me so tightly, I wonder how much strength this little frame can hold.

The rest of the day I can't help but to walk around with a spring in my step and a Cheshire cat smile planted on my face. I am so happy!

Part Two

1

The entire summer grandma has been in and out of hospital, constantly being sick. She is given a tablet each time that stops the sickness temporarily and is sent home. This time mum has asked a doctor to make sure she gets sorted, so that grandma doesn't have to keep going into hospital feeling so ill. It is Thursday, the 11th of August, 2011. This is where it begins.

The hospital has messed gran about so much. Mum and I had to watch her choking as they tried to put a pipe through her nostril and down her throat. She was struggling so much, choking and coughing. The pipe was coming back up out of her mouth and she was nearly sick, all we could do was watch. They couldn't get it down so they tried again when visiting hours were over.

Different tests are being done and we aren't being told the reasons. In the meantime she continues to be sick. I hate watching her suffer. If I could take her place I would in a minute.

She keeps being miss-diagnosed with different things which I try not to get angry about. What I do get angry about however is how neglected some of the patients seem to be, particularly the 'older' patients. A couple of weeks ago we were sat in the day ward with gran. There was a little old lady sat near us who had just received her dinner. It soon dawned on us however, that after watching the lady for some time, try and fail to get food on her fork that she was in fact blind. The lady gave up on eating and put her fork down on to the table. My mum went to her and asked if she needed help, she said that would be very kind of her and my mum set to work feeding the lady. I would be content with the knowledge of her just missing out on a meal because the staff were too busy to help, had I not seen a nurse on the same ward speaking to her daughter on the phone, informing her of jobs she was looking at online that very second.

Another incident I remember involved another old lady who had been put into a bed at the end of the ward. A doctor came in and shouted to her that if she was to stop breathing she was not going to be resuscitated. The lady had a breathing mask on at this moment, she tried to take it off to either agree or voice her objections. However she couldn't remove the mask quickly enough, so she gave up and simply nodded.

We have been told that gran will have another scan tomorrow, but this has now been put back three days. She looks so small and frail in the hospital bed. On weekends nothing is done because there aren't many doctors working. So let's hope I never get ill on a Saturday.

Mum and myself take it in turns to go see grandad, he is very confused, being home alone without grandma there with him. We don't think we can take him in to visit her as he will probably cause a scene. He suffers from dementia so therefore forgets things. He does incredibly well remembering his life from years ago. Recent times however are more difficult to recall.

He can be quite rude and tends to argue with us when frustrated. We tell him grandma will be out soon, we just hope the doctors will get her better.

She has been moved from ward to ward as she was being diagnosed from one illness to another. Eventually she was told she had diverticulitis and that seemed to be the end of it. My mum and gran even celebrated that it was nothing more serious . . .

Several times grandma has asked for a glass of water and was ignored each time. She asked for help to the bathroom, still being ignored she attempted to get there herself. She fell over, unable to find her strength, bruising herself badly.

Not long ago I was watching a nurse attempt to take some of grans blood but she was struggling to find an obliging vein. My grandma was in such pain, hiding her face in my mum's shoulder and crying. The nurse was only doing her job but I wanted to scream and kick her away. Anything to stop my grandma going through this pain. How I kept still, I will never know. Why is this happening, why is my grandma suffering! I want everyone to stop and just leave her now. We want her home where we can look after her. The nurse continued to stab the needle into grandma's arm. Still no blood, we watched helplessly again and again. Please God stop this agony.

I can't think of anything more horrible than watching your loved ones in pain. Knowing there is nothing you can do, but to look on helplessly. Wishing so desperately, you could take their place instead.

Every day we make sure grandad is okay. We feed him; we feed their beautiful dog Lucy. We tell him every day that grandma will be home soon. She's fine. She's okay.

We visit grandma twice a day. She is so fed up. Some of the staff members are very rude to us. We try to be patient. We are more patient than most of the people in the hospital. We don't shout at them like idiots. We aren't rude or disrespectful. We wait for answers. Just hoping grandma is okay. But no one has any answers. No one is telling us what is happening. Nurses ignore us, telling us politely to fuck off sometimes. I don't want to insult every staff member in the hospital. They aren't all terrible. I guess we are just stupidly unlucky to get most of the bad ones.

So many new things happen every day and I wish to God I could remember each thing. I can't though. We are all in limbo. It's like just before a storm is about to hit. You prepare everything you may or may not need. You sit in between the choices off escaping or staying put, hoping your house will be strong enough to survive the beating. Dark clouds swarm above us. It is summer but I see no sunshine.

I am in the local paper with my college results. We bring in the article to grandma and she is so happy. She is showing the results to every random person in the vicinity. She repeats, "This is my granddaughter, she's in the paper. She did brilliant in her exams."

She likes to ask me a lot if I have found myself a man yet. I repeat no, if pigs learn how to fly maybe that's when I will find someone right for me. She is quite scared that I will end up alone. That doesn't scare me as much as you may think. Of course I would like to find somebody, but we live in a different time from people her age. Once you needed a man to survive; now you just need to think like one.

We say goodbye to her. I give her a kiss, my hand lingers on her head. She has such fluffy, white hair. My little cotton bud. I love her so much. I can't wait till she gets out of this horrible place and is back home with us. We will have to go to Bury Market. She likes to get wool for her knitting, and buy me delicious whinberry pies.

We will go to the park soon also. When autumn arrives we will have to collect conkers. I can't wait for her to come home.

We return to the car, but I can't shake off this dark feeling. Maybe it's the storm sensation again. I look up at the sky; the clouds are dark and spooky looking. Yes, must be a storm brewing.

We drive home, but as the night wears on the feeling just gets worse. Such dark anxiety pricks repeatedly at my mind. I cry, begging for God's help. Why am I being like this? Why am I asking for help? It will be nothing, I am just being stupid. Stupid . . .

2

The phone rings. I sit up in bed, still half asleep. For some reason I feel tension, fear. Cold dread settles heavily in my chest. Why do I feel so fearful? Who the hell is on that phone? I stand up and walk to my bedroom door. As I walk through it I hear my mum scream out. I run down the stairs nearly falling down them in the process. I charge into the lounge and see my mum on the phone, crying. Ffyona and I kneel on the floor in front of her waiting anxiously for answers . . .

3

'A year ago today, I cried to God, begging him to let grandma be alright. Nine hours later doctors went to my grandma and told her, without family or anyone there to support her, that she had terminal cancer and that there was nothing they could do. A year ago today.'

4

Ever cried so much you threw up? Crying so deeply you can't even keep your stomach calm? Mum is in the kitchen sobbing. Ffyona is with her. How can our world have fallen so low in such a short space of time?

Dad is saying we must all be strong when we see grandma. I don't know how I can be, but I must. I must be strong for gran. I can't imagine how she is feeling. She has lost all her siblings to cancer.

We take the longest walk through the hospital halls. Everything is dark. I can't recall if it is raining outside. It feels like it is. I don't see the faces of the people walking past me. I feel so numb. So cold. I'm scared to walk through the double doors leading into the ward. My steps feel heavier, or is that just my heart?

She is just lying there in the bed, looking so small and fragile. I have to be strong. We just talk, talk about normal day to day things. She's trying to be strong, but in her unguarded moments I look into her eyes. She has given up. Already she looks like there is nothing more now. I can't bear to look into those eyes when she talks to me. I can't watch her pain, and I can't let her see mine.

Eventually we have to leave. We keep waving back, right up to the double doors. We leave her there, so alone, so scared. I don't want her to be alone. I don't want her to be scared anymore.

5

Grandma is home, her home anyway. The doctors said there is nothing more they could do. She might as well be home where she is comfortable.

We are trying to get as much food down her as possible. We get there every breakfast, lunch and dinner time. We have managed to get grandad in at a day care centre. This gives him a break from the sudden upheaval that has entered his life. It gives us a break from the anger and confusion, he directs to his family.

Mum is looking at all types of food and vitamins that can help fight against cancer. Grandma is taking everything given to her. All the medication she is on is making food taste awful to her. She says everything tastes like metal. She is trying so hard though. We are feeding her egg breakfasts and salmon on toast, her favourites. We are moving on to spicier food, in the hope they take the bad taste away.

A nurse is on the war path with the hospital or doctors or some place that exists to keep us healthy. She needs a signature so she can give grandma an injection for her now double deep vein thrombosis (DVT). This should all have been sorted when we left hospital. She got the DVT when she was in hospital and we weren't told that it was in both legs. She is still sick so we keep calling out doctors for more of the anti-sickness injection. The first type of medication didn't work so she has been moved onto something stronger. It is hard looking after her when grandad is here. He asks her every ten minutes if she wants a cup of tea, cup of tea, cup of tea, always asking if she wants a cup of tea. When mum tells him she doesn't he snaps at her, and when she shouts back he just sneers and laughs at her.

6

Today I decided to surprise her. I had gone on a personalised gift website, and one of the gifts you can get is to name a star after someone. I could not think of anything more fitting than for my grandma to be a beautiful, shining star. I had received the box and took it to her. I don't know if she will still be here by Christmas, but just in case she isn't . . . I want her to have this as a present from me.

I try and distract her thoughts and make her smile, with a film that was practically made to make people smile. I put on Mamma Mia, and I lie on the bed next to her so we can sing along. It doesn't seem to work though. Nothing can distract her mind from the thoughts, the fears. Cancer has taken over her mind more than the cancerous parts of her body.

They don't know exactly where the cancer started from. Only that it has probably spread through the bowel and possibly up to the lungs. All the blood tests she had done, and it was never detected.

I so desperately want to take her to the park, so we can collect our conkers. She will not leave her room now though. Our friends from Aultbea have come to see her, Dougie and Margaret-Ann. She is trying hard to be polite and happy but she doesn't like people seeing her like this. Our friends are being so lovely and understanding though, and I cannot thank them enough.

7

Every day is a battle. Whilst mum stays with gran, I go from pharmacy to pharmacy getting her medication. Some places don't do certain types so I have to go to others instead. If they don't have it I go to the hospital. Every day is a routine, feeding grandma, trying to feed ourselves. Watching her sleep, trying to sleep also.

Sometimes I just sit there and watch her sleep, looking so calm and peaceful. I watch her chest rise up and down as she takes each breath. Here is where I cry. So quietly, so silently so she won't hear. Each day she gets weaker. I can see the bones in her arms and legs now.

Her knees are bruised from where she keeps falling. That's another common thing. Grandad will try to open the front door and usually cannot find the key. So he shouts up to grandma to help him find it. He doesn't stop shouting until she does. She wants so desperately to just sleep, so she tries to find the key to keep him quiet. But like I say, she is weak. She falls to the floor heavily, crying and shouting for help. When no one hears her, she reaches for the phone and dials our home number. We get there as fast as we can, but she is in so much pain we are scared to lift her and make it worse. We are forced to call for an ambulance so the paramedics can help. They get her back into bed so she can rest. I rub cream over her bruises. I apply it so gently; frightened I will hurt her more.

8

I have a thing for her to eat at the moment. A little plate covered with slices of cheese, ham and tomatoes. It is the only thing she enjoys eating so I have christened them 'Bella snacks' after myself and I feed them to her. I hold them to her lips and she slowly opens her mouth. She chews little bits, and looks into my eyes. This is how we communicate a lot of the time now, saying everything we want to say but what we can't bring ourselves to speak out loud.

I took out some of her homemade vegetable soup and re-heated it on the stove. If I had known that she was going to make this her last meal, I would have made her something more extravagant.

She has decided to stop the medication and stop eating. She just wants to go now, and I have to accept this as much as I can. My grandma is dying, and there is nothing I can do about it.

Her cheek bones are more prominent. She sleeps a lot, waiting for the last day. She gave up the moment she heard those words uttered. People don't need to die from cancer, but it is too far along for her to be saved. She is too old and weak to be treated. The doctor was as kind as he could be when he told us that. She is at an age where it could just make her worse. On the subject of age however

I hate how many times I hear people say, 'well she's had a good life'. No she hasn't, and I wish I could be more grateful for the length of her life but I cannot be right now. I know the pains she has faced and I see another type of pain now. Age shouldn't matter, shouldn't a cure for any age, size, race, be the most important statements spoken. Yes she is older, but she is still a mum, a grandma, a wife. Age does not make the pain any easier to deal with.

A man from a cancer charity turned up. As helpful as the organisation is this man was not. All he could do was sip his tea and say to my grandma, "Oh what are we going to do with you, you're a problem you are." I wanted to lash out at him for saying that to her.

A nurse from somewhere else has arrived. My mum asks him if they should turn my gran over in bed. He tells her not too and to just leave her where she is comfortable. This is the wrong thing to do, even if she were to feel a lot of pain. When a district nurse came round, mum asked her the same question, to which she demanded of course they must turn her over. The sight when they did was shocking. My grandma was bruised all the way down from her shoulder, her arm, down the length of her hip and leg right to her ankles. I wish I could exaggerate how much blue and green I could see on her body, but I cannot. She looked like a paint pallet, and I was disgusted at how painful they must have felt. Disgusted, that the experts suddenly jumping into our lives, were failing us so miserably.

We managed to get grandad in almost every day at the care centre. It was good to have him out I must admit.

I do love him but at times he can be the nastiest man alive. He has always had a nasty side, and always shown most of it to grandma. He does love her, he can't live without her. But is love so twisted that we as humans can treat the ones we love with such nastiness and cruelty, and accept it as love being that way? Mum says that's how it was with the oldies. I don't want to believe that though. I don't want to believe that love is as toxic as people make out. I think people can be toxic, and we can blame it on loving and caring for them too much.

A doctor from the hospital has left in suspicious circumstances and all his records have miraculously disappeared with him. I don't know how that can happen, but this doctor had been dealing with grandma.

Doctors keep apologising to us. We have been told that the system is a sham by the staff themselves. The hospitals and care in the community aren't what they should be; all this has been said by the doctors.

Grandad is so confused with it all. We keep telling him she is dying and he cries with pain and heartbreak. But in five minutes he forgets. It breaks us like nothing could, having to utter these words each time, so sometimes we don't. We just say she is not well. We hate lying but we can't stand the tears and grief each time. We don't want to hurt him, and we can't keep hurting ourselves. Is the blissful ignorance sometimes better than the painful truth? He will know someday. One day he will wake up, alone in bed. That will be all the truth he needs.

9

I'm so numb now. I don't know what else to tell you. Every day I let the nurses in, and watch them fill in a form and comment on her condition. Every day we tell grandad that his wife is ill, meeting him from the centre and making him a cup of coffee, then his dinner. I watch the murder mysteries on TV with him. I try and distract myself with the programmes. Poirot and Midsomer Murders have truly saved my mind recently. Grandad asks me regularly if I would like a cup of tea. "No grandad I don't like tea."

"How about coffee?"

"No thank you grandad I don't like coffee either."

"What do you drink then?"

"Water, juice, milk, (vodka)."

"Well do you want some milk? There should be some juice in."

"No I'm okay, but thank you for asking grandad."

Every night I cry myself to sleep. I yell at God asking him why he's done this. Then I tell him I'm sorry for blaming him. Then I cry again begging him to help us. I don't know why I've taken this sudden interest in speaking to God constantly. I feel like he is the only one I can talk too. The only one that can listen. The only one that can help if he so chooses. I beg, I plead, I yell, I cry.

When my tears run out, I ask him to stay with grandma, and make sure she is not too scared.

We wake up with the phone ringing. Grandma was on the floor again, she had fallen trying to get the keys for grandad. Mum went down to try and lift her up but she couldn't. She was like a dead weight. We called for an ambulance and the paramedics helped her back into bed. Grandad was abusive to them and to mum as well. He is making the situation so much more difficult.

The paramedic told us about how crap the system is. If it was just our family becoming bitter and angry about life I would understand if people didn't take us seriously. But it is the staff in the profession themselves who agree! We hear it from them and are shocked. The years my grandma gave to this country, am I selfish in wanting better for her? Better than this?

I watch her sleep all the time. She barely talks now. She has been fitted with a catheter, so she no longer needs to move. We moved grandad into the other room so he can sleep peacefully. Mum is with her all day and most of the night. I hate to think how she must be feeling. Grandma is so special, I know I'm biased but I do mean it. She brought us up, becoming another mum. She is such a good person, and it is so rare to find a truly good person nowadays.

"You go home I'll watch over her now." I tell mum.

"Are you sure?" She looks exhausted and devastated. How could she not be?

"Yeah, go on, go eat or sleep." She stands up to leave, and gives me a hug.

"I love her so much."

"I love her too.

"Why did this have to happen?" I don't know. I will never know.

I sit in the chair at the corner of the room and watch over this little, fragile form in the bed. I say to myself at least she is still here; she is still here with you. I thank God for that at least. My head is constantly sore from trying not to cry. My heart feels broken completely.

I am meant to be spending my first months in university but I have only been in every other few days. I am not a favourite with the tutors but I don't care right now. One day I went in and I spent an hour in a lecture. I found the lecture so pointless, if it had been under normal circumstances I would have just listened and got on with it. But I was just angry, angry that I was listening to such shit, when I could have been spending the time with my grandma. I stormed out and drove home. I became quite arrogant and decided to only go in when I felt it was important enough. One tutor however, Tracy, was kind enough to accept my predicament, and let me have as much time as I needed. I'm sure she didn't mean for most of the time, but I decided to take up the offer anyway.

Every day gets harder. I have become a full time carer at eighteen. I don't complain though, there are kids younger than me caring for family members. I leave late at night but arrive back later in the morning each day. Mum is there constantly of course. We are taking it in turns to watch over her. Someone must be there to let the nurses into the house. They ask me questions I can't answer but I do my best. They don't stay long, so I sit in my chair and watch her again.

The phone rings and I have to get it at lightning speed so the sound doesn't wake gran. Bloody PPI calls. I throw the phone down in frustration. I watch and wait for anything else to happen. I try and read a book but my mind can't focus on the pages. Every time it seems like grandma has gone still, my heart stops, but she moves again and I sag with relief.

My friends ask if I can meet up with them but it's very rare that I can. Life has become a ticking time bomb and any minute it will explode. I have lost count of how many friends I have lost now. They think I'm not as busy as I say I am. I only wish they never get the chance to go through this. I do envy some of them though. Most of us have started university and I see some of them post on Facebook how happy they are, and how perfect life currently is. I feel quite bitter and angry at their happiness. I know I shouldn't, and as I realise these dark feelings I exile them from my mind immediately. I cannot begrudge them their happiness. They are living their lives and I should not dislike them for it. I only wish one of them would look down from their wonderful towers of happiness and look at the people crawling through the shit on the floor, and offer them a helping hand. Only a few friends will do that now, and I have to accept this as much as I can.

Gran has stopped talking. I don't understand where her voice has gone. Maybe she is so weak that even speaking is too difficult. We talk to her and she listens. I look into her eyes and wonder what she is saying to me. I want to tell her so many things, but by saying them I would be telling her goodbye. And I am not ready for goodbyes just yet. I never will be. I just look back at her and tell her through my eyes how much I love her. How much she means to me. I tell her I'm sorry for the times I ignored her. For upsetting her and worrying her when I was at my lowest with depression.

How I miss the days we would watch TV lying on the bed. How much I would miss going to her for dinner, and laugh at how many servings she gave me. She would always make me curry and rice because that was my favourite. She would go out especially just to get it for me.

I thank her for being so patient with me when she was teaching me how to knit cardigans. Thank her for always supporting me, every minute of my life. I have so many things to thank her for. I never thanked her enough. I was never grateful enough for having her in my life. Always be grateful for every blessing in your life. You never know when it will be taken away.

I say all this with my eyes. I say it to her eyes. I tell her I love her again. I tell her that I am going to miss her. The very thought of life without her tears my heart apart. I hold her hand, and I watch her go back to sleep.

Dad has asked me to drive him to see gran. We don't think it will be long now. I watch him, from my chair at the bottom of the room, sit beside her and talk to her.

"Just been watching the footie. United won against shitty City. So that wasn't too bad." He stares at grandma. She became like a mother to him. When mum and dad were younger, if they ever argued, dad would go running off to grandma. She would proceed to feed him and tell him how wonderful he was and not to worry about mum; she just needed a chill pill. Even though mum is her daughter, she still made space for my dad in her heart.

He puts on a Scottish accent for her, mimicking how she would be calling him a silly prick right now. It looks like she smiles but we can't be sure if that is us just hoping.

I have never seen my dad look so broken and it kills me to watch. He asks me if I could leave him alone and pick him up later. I come back for him and he has been crying. He has said all he wanted to say. I beg silently to the air, please don't take her from us. Please don't take her away from me.

10

Ffyona and I have gone back to another pharmacy to get some more medication. This one will keep her calm and relax her in her final hours. We sit and wait for them to call our grandmas name. It seems to take forever.

Eventually they do and I drive us home.

"Do you want to come with me?" I ask her.

"Err, no its okay I will go tomorrow." She walks into the house in a trance like state. I reluctantly get back into the car and drive straight to my grans house where mum is waiting.

I open the front door and walk into the hallway. All of a sudden I hear my mum scream at somebody. I run up to gran. I see her gulping and making a choking sound. A nurse is there with her trying to keep her calm. Mum is screaming at someone to come and help.

"It's fucking ridiculous. There's no one available to give her the medication. No one will come out."

"What?" I ask, sudden anger swelling through me.

"It's ridiculous I . . . One second." Someone must have started speaking.

"Hello, I need someone out here; I've been passed from pillow to post and no one will fucking help us . . . No I won't calm down! I . . . No, why can't *you* speak to me? . . . I need somebo . . . FOR FUCK SAKE!" They must have put her on hold. I sit down next to grandma. What is wrong with her? I hear mum shouting for help again.

No one is available to administer the medication I had just picked up. The day nurses have finished and the night nurses won't start for another hour. Mum is screaming at doctors but they are passing her on constantly. I hold grandmas hand. I'm so scared.

"Keep her calm! Make sure she's okay!" Mum shouts to me through angry tears. I don't know what to say.

"Grandma, please breathe, it's okay, it's going to be okay, just relax, you will be okay I promise." She looks at me; her eyes wild with fear. Her mouth opens and closes like a fish in the open air, fighting desperately for oxygen. I hold her and cry. Looking into her eyes, wishing the fear would leave them.

"Please grandma, please don't be scared, you will be okay, just breathe for me gran!" She makes more terrible sounds, such awful, choking sounds.

"WHAT'S WRONG WITH HER? WHAT'S HAPPENING?"

The nurse is looking at me; something has entered her eyes. Resignation? Pity? Grief? I look away from her and back to my grandma. God what is happening? Please God save her! Stop this pain! Why won't you stop this pain! Another choking sound. Gasping. Wretched gasping. Jagged breaths, in and out. Please, please help her!

"Go get your mum." Was that the nurse speaking? I stare at her in shock, unable to move from grandma's side. "Go get your mum!" She yells at me and I run to my mum, she hangs up the phone and follows me back to gran. I sit on the chair next to my grandma telling her to breathe.

Everything halts . . . The choking sound has disappeared, she has stopped moving. We are so still. The nurse moves her hand towards her but then grandma makes a sudden movement. I cannot describe to you how immense the relief was, but it feels larger than what the universe must be. In seconds I was thanking everyone I could and begging them to carry on. But suddenly she stops again. My heart sinks and I hope with every fibre of my body that this isn't it.

The nurse brings her hand to my grandma's neck and feels for the pulse, the most important pulse I need to keep my life going. I see a tear roll down her cheek. She looks up at us, "I'm sorry."

11

I'm screaming, screaming and crying. Mum is over grandma, calling out mummy. Begging her to come back to her. I am crying out to grandma. Begging her not to leave us. I hold her hand to my cheek. Wishing her fingers could wrap around mine and tell me it is all okay. Screaming and choking on my tears. "Please come back."

Mum is holding her. I'm walking around the room wishing I could find cancer and kill it. Wishing I could slaughter all the people who had let her down. Who let her go the way she did.

I stare at grandma, hoping it is all just a nightmare. Mum has her head resting on grandma's chest. She is sobbing and begging for her to come back.

"Please mummy, please don't leave me! She cries.

I scream silently to the air watching her. Screaming pain out from my body, too tortured to make a sound. If I could rip out my heart would it stop this unbearable pain?

Mum tells me to go to Jean and Fred next door and I run to them. Jean holds me and I cry onto her shoulder. I cry so much I can't breathe. Fred is crying in the other room. I can't stay long I need to go back. I need to see my grandma.

Her body is cold now. It is so cold. I just stare at the fragile little body. There are still the bruises left from the times she fell. The small holes where all the needles were put in. That poor little body. I touch the beautiful ball of hair on her head. So white and cute, my little cotton bud. Her eyes are blank. There is nothing there. I put my head on hers and cry more. Begging her to come back. "Come back grandma, please come back to me."

I somehow drive home. I park on the driveway and get out of my car. Jon runs to me and I collapse screaming in his arms. He carries me inside and I hold Fe as we cry on to one another.

She went, in pain. Because there was no one available to give her the medication.

I watched my beautiful grandma die. I held her as she took her last breath.

My grandma is dead.

12

I slowly put on my black dress. It fits tightly to my body, gradually flowing out around my knees. I look into the mirror and examine myself. 'You look like shit Annabella.' I know I do. I attempt to style my hair and put on make-up. I decided that though I don't want to be making myself up at all, I want to look special for grandma. She would have wanted that.

I greet people at the door, my mum's cousin and her family from Edinburgh arrive. Her cousin Helen lost her six year old grandson to cancer, only a few weeks ago. Jean and Fred from next door arrive, Alec, Margaret-Ann and Dougie from Aultbea. Other people arrive, so many I can't remember them all. I feel such gratitude for them all taking the time out to be here.

I dread the moment till we have to leave. I'm talking and smiling, remarkably being a rather good hostess. Everyone talks about gran. They say how much they are going to miss her. Some turn their heads to wipe away the tears from their eyes. I don't know what to say back. Probably nothing. I just smile and look down, not trusting myself to speak. I feel like my soul could drown in sorrow. I've cried so many tears I feel they could create a tsunami the size of America. I pray every night to let it all just be a dream. But in the morning I wake, and the reality attacks me violently. She's gone. My beautiful grandma has gone.

The Hurst pulls up outside the house. I see the coffin, so beautifully presented, covered in flowers. That is when it hits me. That is when I begin to weep. Her little body is laid out in that box. I feel like I can't get enough air into my lungs. My friend Dan holds me and tells me it will be okay. I begin to relax, and inhale the breaths of strength needed to get me through this day.

I climb into the car next to Fe and Jon. Mum, grandad and dad are sat in front of us. We have a lovely man in charge called Simon, who is dressed so smartly I feel we have gone back a century. He walks in front of the cars, taking us down to the bottom of the street. He bows his head at my grandma's coffin, and then gets into the car.

People in the cars behind are very patient with us going at a slow speed. Every so often a pedestrian stops walking and bows his or her head. I thank them silently for showing respect, something we don't see much of nowadays.

We gradually pull up to the chapel. It is strange that grandma would pick this place to be buried, as she has never been here before. But she made a good choice. The chapel is beautiful, made from old stone with a large steeple on top. Trees and flowers surround it, casting a picturesque touch to the scene. The sun has come out and even through my grief I can see how beautiful the day is.

My dad holds me up as we follow the coffin through the chapel. I can't bear to look at this box any longer. I can't bear it knowing that she is in there, and I will never see her again.

We take our seats and I manage to inspect the chapel a bit more as people file in after us. The chapel is so quaint, with pictures of Jesus and the Virgin Mary painted all over. A large cross hangs from the wall, right between my grandmas' coffin. Candles are lit everywhere, illuminating the stained glass windows.

An old man, who I recognise to be the minister, steps forward and thanks us all for being here. We sing hymns and read from the bible. I cannot remember exactly what the minister says but I know it all makes perfect sense. I remember him telling us that grandma, (Annabella, also her name) was someone who could always make you smile, and how she was the sunshine in everybody's day. How kind and caring she was to people, how she was a true angel, who loved us all so dearly. He spoke so accurately of her I wondered how he knew this without ever meeting her.

It was then my turn to stand at the front and read my poem. I was so ill, coughing constantly. My dad helped me up and Ffyona stood alongside me. I tried to remember a decade of acting lessons, and force myself not to cry. I even did something silly and projected my voice, as I was taught in college, so that everyone could hear me.

I took a breath, and then another. And then I began my poem.

It seems like the earth should stop spinning
Like the sun should never shine
That time should freeze in place
So you could always be mine

You taught me how to be strong
To love and forgive
Taught me how to care
Taught me how to live

Taught me how to stand on my own two feet
Taught me to never give up
To never ever be beat

You passed true life's test grandma
You were perfect in every way
You must know how much we miss you
How we love you more each day

I know that with every star that shines
Every raindrop that falls
Every rose bud that blooms
These miracles will be yours

Let us remember you as the angel of our earth
The kindest grandma, our family could deserve
The little cotton bud we fought to protect
The beautiful woman I shall never forget

So for now we must say goodnight
But never ever goodbye
I love you with all my heart
My angel, my beautiful grandma

The minister congratulated me and I walked back to my seat. I could see people crying, not at my poetry skills but because the words were true. We had fought with everyone in the last months of grandma's life. We had been disappointed by the very people who should not have let us down. A part of all of us had vanished that night, and she was the kindest, sweetest, dearest part of lives. Now that part of us had gone.

The Scottish tradition is for the male members of the family to hold the chords that would lower the coffin into the ground. Dad and my brother were amongst the other brave men who helped lower grandma into the grave. I was very proud of Jon; I can't imagine how he felt having to do that.

When the minister had said his words, the family members threw rose petals onto the coffin. The image of that box, down at the bottom of that pit still haunts my mind. My grandma, she is down there.

We weep more as the procession begins to travel back to the cars. I don't want to leave her. I don't want to leave her alone. She is no longer in pain, but she is no longer with us. God help me to get through this. Help us all to get through this.

13

Every day we wake up and try to carry on as normal. As a family we have to stick together. We try to make each other smile, try to distract each other's minds. But the pain is as raw as our flesh. Stabbing us with long, deliberate thrusts.

Dad goes to work every day. Mum and I take it in turns to look after grandad. Fe has to go to college and keep on working. Jon has to meet social workers and continue to get his life back on track. Every night we cry ourselves to sleep. What the hell happened to us?

I keep seeing her face. Seeing her eyes. I can hear that sound she made as she took her last breath. I see it all the time. I ask a vacant spirit why my grandma had to go. I am left alone in the darkness. Waiting for an answer that will never come.

I am sat in the kitchen playing music out load from my iPod. I am giving each one of my family members their own theme tune. Mum is 'Clair de Lune' by Claude Debussy as that's her favourite piece of music. I give dad something silly like 'I'm too sexy' and he gives us a little catwalk routine.

We are beginning to find reasons to laugh again. It has only been three weeks since grandma died. But we are trying to find reasons to carry on. I feel grateful for the people around this table. Grateful that I can call them my family. I go to bed feeling happier. But good things don't always last do they?

14

I sit in one lounge whilst dad sits in the other. We are watching separate shows on TV. I mind my own business as I chat to my friends on Facebook. My dad walks in, it looks like he has been crying. But that can't be, dad doesn't cry.

"What's wrong?" I ask him.

"Nothing. Please don't hate me. Please don't ever hate me."

I sit forward and stare at him in astonishment. "I could never hate you daddy."

"You may soon, but you must know how much I love you. Please don't hate me." I can only stare on in silence. Wishing desperately he would tell me what he was going on about. But he isn't going to talk. It is near impossible to get information out of my dad, if he wishes to keep it hidden. I am so worried. He looks at me pleading with his eyes. Begging me not to hate him. I tell him we may fight, but I could never hate him.

He gives me a kiss goodnight, and I am left alone in fear. What is my daddy going to do, that may cause me to hate him. I go to bed, and cry again to God. Asking him for help. I ask him to do what is best for us, but to give us strength to carry on through it. The next day I find my answer.

15

I get Fe and Jon into the car and take them out for a drive. This is no casual drive; we have to leave the house for a while. As we drive round Bury, our town, our dad is putting his bags into his car. Leaving his home for good. His feelings had changed. He was no longer happy. He tried for so long to keep up a charade. But he could no longer act. Acting was my job, not his.

For three weeks we lived in a constant terrible atmosphere. Mum too devastated to talk to dad. 'The children' going from one parent to the other. Trying to keep things as normal as possible. We are a broken family. All drowning in our individual pools of despair.

When I feel enough time has gone by I take my sister and brother back to the street where we live. I am driving at a snail's pace. Fearful of what we will see. My daddy's car has gone. He has gone. He has moved out of his home, our home. Our family will never be the same again. Mummy is crying in the living room. Ffyona goes to hug her. I close my eyes, hoping this year has just been a long dream. It has not. My mummy is devastated. My daddy has gone. We have joined the ranks of broken families everywhere.

"I'm so sorry for doing this. I just don't know what else to do. I need to be happy, and I think you will all be happier without me too." My dad cried to me saying these words, and I held him wishing I could take away his hurt. I wish I could have told him to stay, but I didn't want to see him unhappy. I would have liked to be the troublesome teen and shout with hatred. But I looked into his eyes, and knew he was sorry. He wished he did not feel like this. But sometimes we are beyond our own control.

I think about the childhood he had. His father walking out on him when he was a child. Never being told that he was loved. Living in near enough complete poverty. Working so hard to make sure his kids would have the childhood he never had.

We cried on each other, taking turns to say how much we loved one another. My dad and I are so similar. This hasn't always been a good thing; being so similar makes us argue and fight. You would think World War III had been declared when we disagree. But there is that connection, neither of us can escape from.

I tell him I love him, how I could never hate him. We hold each other till the tears stop. I leave him to watch TV so I can get to bed. This will be the last night that my daddy and I can cry together; in the place that was once his home.

My parents have separated. My mum is alone. My life has broken into thousands of pieces. I don't care about anything anymore.

16

Mum is spending every day at grandads. So am I really. I am meant to be in university but I don't give a damn about anything at the moment. I've lost more friends and as much as I'd like to be upset about that I can't be. How can anyone understand unless they know exactly how it feels? I want to build a sign that tells the entire world to piss off! Don't pretend to care when I know you don't give a damn!

I escape to grandad's house whilst he is at the centre. I hold Lucy and watch her play. Lucy is, was grandma's dog. She is the only life on earth that is not harsh or cruel. Most animals are like that, that is why I get on better with them than people. I hold her in my lap and let my own pain ebb away. You may think it is stupid but I start to feel sorry for her, this little dog in my lap. She has dealt with strangers in her home and her owner leaving her forever. Now she is left alone all day in this cold house, and having to be cared for by grandad. We think she should go somewhere else, but that would mean taking everyone away from grandad. She may just be a dog but she is my grandad's only friend.

Within a week it is Christmas. I am trying so desperately to make this one good. Even though it will be the worst Christmas we have ever known. Mum has still made Christmas dinner for her old friend Jack. This time I will take it to him though.

We pick up grandad and bring him to our house. We have to tell him again that his wife is dead. Each day for two months we have had to repeat to him this news. Each day he cries and begins to grieve all over again. Can you imagine finding out that the one you love is dead, and you cannot remember it? You can't remember their funeral, and saying goodbye.

He asks us every day how she died. We tell him cancer. He asks us if she went peacefully, we lie. He takes out the handkerchief from his pocket, and dries his eyes. I just put the TV on hoping to distract his mind.

He has his lovely Christmas dinner, and opens his presents. We then have to take him back home. Our own dinner becomes dust in our mouths. Grandad is alone, without his wife, for the first time in sixty years.

Grandma is not here with us, making us smile, making us feel loved. Mum is distraught, her mum, her best friend, has gone. Her dad is alone. She is alone. She begins to drink, hoping the alcohol will numb the pain. But it doesn't. It hides it for a few hours. In the morning it will return. More devastating and destroying than before.

I'm back in bed now, crying into my pillow, crying till my face is red and my throat is sore. Please help me God; I don't think I can do this anymore.

17

January goes by, much the same as usual. February arrives and I decide to go back into university. The first day I am in, I have been given the wrong timetable. I wander the halls looking for my class, to no avail. I try to find a teacher to ask for help but no one seems to know where I am meant to be. I start to cry in frustration and race to my car. I get in and slam the door, dropping my head against the steering wheel. This just isn't going to work. If my circumstances were different I may be able to manage it, but I can't. I am ill, mentally and physically. I am a full time carer along with my mum, and we have no money. Jon is trying to find work, but it's difficult with his conditions. Mum is fragile and cannot bear to keep telling her father that his wife, her mum, is dead. She cannot grieve, and she is alone. We are trying to keep Ffyona's life as normal as possible. She shouldn't have to deal with all this shit.

Our house is up for sale. We could no longer afford it. Actually, we could never really afford it. I don't know what will happen to us. First our loved ones, then ourselves, now our home. What has happened?

I am almost always with grandad, and finding work will be difficult. I look for night jobs but it is through the night that grandad will phone, asking where grandma is. We live in constant fear, wondering if he will go out and wander the streets looking for her. Life has become this dull, constant, painful routine.

18

<u>March</u>

Mum—Dad phoned four times in the night, 3am-3.45-5am-5.30. So abusive to me. Saying, "Oh I'm sorry for phoning but you won't forgive me. You're nasty always have been."

What have I done to deserve this! I don't know what to do. In the space of three months I've lost my mum and best friend, my husband. I'm losing my house. What next? I can't feel any lower than I do today.

Me—Grandad keeps calling. I'm feeling so tired, well more than usual. Mum isn't well and it's not helping her that she can't sleep because of grandad phoning. Every night I fear the phone ringing. I feel so anxious, just waiting for more bad news.

Mum—I wake up nearly every morning thinking if it wasn't for my babies.

Mum—Been thinking of mum a lot today. She loved this time of year. She would be starting her spring cleaning now and getting her garden ready for summer. Oh God I wish she was still here.

April

Mum—Jean phoned me at 9am to tell me dad was knocking at her door at 1.30 in the morning. I just don't know what to do!

Me—Grandad has a routine now of waking up his neighbours at stupid times in the morning. He is waking up and looking for grandma, realising she is not lay beside him. Mum's friend found him again wandering the street; she wasn't sure which house we lived in so she knocked on a couple of houses asking our neighbours where we lived. She eventually found us and handed grandad over to mum. Mum and grandad had a huge argument. I can't really explain how impossible this situation is.

Mum—Woke up crying over mum. I can't believe she isn't here with me. Every dream, every night is about her. Either sat with me, walking round Bury, or watching her die.

Mum—He promised he wouldn't go out after Sue phoned to let me know he had been out at 12.30 in the morning. Then Jean and Fred phoned saying he was in their house looking for mum. I phoned him and went mad. I'm so tired; he needs to go into a home. I can't do this anymore. I feel so depressed. I think I'm having a breakdown.

Me—I am so tired with all this. I feel tired with grandad. I feel so guilty saying that. I love him so much, but I feel so bad about his neighbours being woken up at stupid times, they must be getting sick of it.

I can't be upset with him, I can't. This is dementia. I think I would rather die than have this. It is a disgusting disease, taking the person you love and robbing them from you. You are left with a body, yes very much alive, but no longer the person you love.

He keeps blaming mum for everything, which makes me angry. But when I go and make his dinner I will watch him, sitting there so quiet and lonely. Eating his dinner wondering where his wife is. I don't want to leave him alone, yet everything in my body tells me to escape this house.

I can't go upstairs. I can still see her lay in that bed. Just a body, no soul, growing colder as time goes by. Those empty eyes. Such sad lips, she was so unhappy, so desperately distraught. Sometimes I think the knowledge of cancer killed her more than the actual cancer.

No, this house will never be the same without her. I watch Poirot with grandad again, trying to keep him company for as long as possible. I need to leave soon, I feel claustrophobic with the darkness of this house, this house that was once the source of so much happiness.

I kiss him goodbye and feel guilty as I do so. This situation is impossible. If you could just see how impossible this is! From the moment we heard about the cancer, to this position we find ourselves in now. I feel such guilt, such sadness. I leave my little Lucy feeling guilty for her also.

He waves at me through the window and my throat tightens. Oh this poor man, he will only feel happiness when he is with grandma once more.

April/May

Mum—Jean phoned at 8.40, dad was outside waiting for a taxi. I rushed down, he said some terrible things. He then got on a bus. I had to call the police. They got him not far, on the bus going to Manchester. He was taken to the psychiatric ward in hospital.

Me—Mum was on the phone hysterical, telling me what had happened with grandad waiting for a taxi. I was there in literally five minutes and I could not find him anywhere. I walked round the streets near his house in case I would find him wandering around. The rain was making it difficult to see. I got back and told mum I couldn't find him. What the hell was happening today?

Mum really began to panic then and called his social worker. She told mum to call the police immediately which mum did. We got the biggest, scariest looking policeman I've ever seen! He was really lovely though. We had to fill out a missing persons report. In hindsight the situation was quite hilarious. He told us he would have to just do a search of the house in case he was hiding, we had to laugh. He told us this is usually done if a child has gone missing in case they are just hiding from parents. Obviously grandad wasn't hiding under the bed and they had already called out search teams to look for him. He was eventually found five minutes away on a bus going to Manchester. The social worker told the policeman to arrest him and bring him to the psychiatric ward at the hospital. He told us they weren't going to arrest grandad unless he physically harmed them. It was quite funny imagining grandad taking on this enormous police officer.

We drove to the hospital and found the psychiatric ward he was on. The walls were painted purple and had pictures of smiley faces everywhere. That just freaked me out a bit if I'm honest.

I sat with him and spoke to him but he was so angry. He didn't want to see mum and kept telling me to keep her away. We didn't stay long, after that. We had to be ushered through the door quickly to make sure none of the other patients got out.

I got home and just sat down for a while, frozen with shock. What the hell had just happened today?

<u>May</u>

Mum—Oh God it's my birthday today. I don't wonder why I can't stop crying. Wish mum was here. Can't believe she's gone.

Bella and I went to hospital to see about dad. Don't know if I'm doing the right thing having him away from his home.

Me—Grandad is being really lovely, we are having a great time. It is lovely to see him and mum behaving like father and daughter. We watch a documentary with David Attenborough. We are all amazed at the wonderful wildlife filling up the screen. I have enjoyed this day.

Mum—Went to see _____care home. Have put dad's name on the list. But the price is £550 per week. Don't know how I am going to afford that. Going to make appointment for _____ care home, see if that is nice.

May/June

Me—Got a call from the ward. Grandad has been suffering from chest pains and was rushed to A&E. Mum had drunk some wine so I drove us to the hospital as fast as I could. He looked so small and weak in the bed. We stayed with him whilst the doctors ran some tests. I don't know what time it was getting too, maybe 2-3am.

Things seemed to be okay, so we were told he could go back to the ward. We had to travel back to the other side of the hospital. It's getting near summer but it was freezing tonight. Grandad was shivering and we were putting our coats over him to keep him warm.

We eventually got to the ward and rang the bell for the doors to be opened. A nurse came to the door and told us he couldn't be let back in. The doctor who came up with us went berserk with her. "Why can't he be let back in!?" A form hadn't been signed. The psychiatric ward is a different group from the NHS. Going from one to the other meant a form had to be signed even though grandad had been in the ward just a few hours before. This poor doctor went mad at the nurse and was possibly written up for fighting our corner. It was nice to see someone actually fighting for us.

We took grandad all the way back down to A&E, got the piece of paper signed and took him all the way back up to the ward. I'm angry. I'm tired. When did life become so fucked up?

June

Mum—Went to see dad with Fe. Doctor asked to see me. When we sat down she asked a few questions then asked; if anything was to happen, did I want them to resuscitate him?

Me—He got ill again and had to be moved to another ward. He has been in this ward for eight days. In eight days he has declined so quickly. I did not think it humanly possible for someone to fail so fast. His bones are showing everywhere. Just like grans was. He can't eat. He can't talk. He just lies there. He smiles at us, that is something at least.

We have nurses telling us he is doing well and taking his medication. Yet we see the medication next to him untouched. One nurse actually asked us if we could get it down him as he hadn't taken it, when we tried and failed she simply threw it away.

He looks a mess. He has wasted away to nothing. When we went to visit him he was slouched over the arm of a chair. The staff held him up with pillows around his body, but that was only after we asked for help to sit him up straight. How long had he been sat like this?

Some woman came to ask mum what he could do before he came to the ward. She expected him to not be able to do much for himself. She got the shock of her life when we corrected her! He could walk, talk and jump on buses planning great escapes. Make his drinks-not dinner though that was always grandma's job.

He needs the toilet; we are left waiting for twenty minutes for someone to help him. They hoist him up, and he screams in pain. I don't know why he hasn't been fitted with a catheter. If it takes so long for the nurses to help him go to the toilet, is he being left in the bed to soil himself?

He looks close to death. I think it will happen soon. A nurse has told us he is fit for discharge. Is he fuck! Sorry for the language but he isn't fit to go anywhere at all! If he is okay to leave then he needs to go out the way he came in. Not like this, near death! He is nil by mouth, he has eaten nothing for the last few days. We have asked why he cannot eat and are told to speak to a doctor. When we try to speak to a doctor they are never available to speak to us.

In eight days he looks almost like a skeleton, a skeleton held together only by skin. It is disgraceful the sight I see, and worse, how he got like this in the first place. I think I see pure neglect. I see death being forced onto a man by people who are meant to protect him. Am I exaggerating? Please God say I am. What is going on behind closed doors? What are we not seeing? What is happening when a perfectly healthy man can be brought down to this, in such a short space of time? What have they done to my grandad?

19

It is probably the wrong time to be going away but for my own sanity I must. I feel I am constantly shouting at my family, constantly letting down my friends. I am no help to anyone at the moment, so I must leave. My best friend Angie is living in London at the moment, as she has just spent a year at RADA. This is the only time we are both available so I must go now.

Dad drives me down, and we spend the entire journey laughing and talking. Within a few hours we are there. Angie greets me at the corner and I rush out to hug her. I'm in my country's capital and I'm finally getting away for a while. I say a tearful goodbye to my dad and watch him drive away. Angie helps me with my suitcase and takes me up to her rooms.

I sit on the bed and stare out at London. For the first time in ten months I breathe out a sigh of relief. Maybe just for a few days I can pretend nothing has happened. Maybe I can let the city, take away my pain, just for a short while. I unpack my case and start my city adventure.

Angie shows me London and I love the place already. However I remember my previous conclusions that I completely despise the tube as it is far too hot and my personal space is been invaded far more than I would like it to be.

The second day I am there, we go on a museum spree. We go to the Natural History Museum and I am blown away with how wonderful our natural world is. We then go to the Victoria and Albert museum and look at the fashion through the ages. I decide that clothes from the past are so much more beautiful than the clothes we wear now.

I walk through rooms decorated as they would have been in the Victorian era, and admire the beauty of that time. We walk through a hallway lined with sculptures and I can almost imagine being Keira Knightly in the film Pride and Prejudice.

20

Mum got the phone call early in the morning. "Come quick he hasn't got long." When she got there all the doors were locked. She had to run to the other side of the hospital, all the way through the corridors back to the other side to his ward.

She had just missed him. He had been put in a room on his own. His eyes were still open. Mum thought he was still alive, but he wasn't. She closed his eyes and sat next to him holding his hand. Her mum and now her dad, it hasn't even been a year.

Missed calls from mummy. I grab the phone, rubbing away at my sleepy eyes. I find her name in the address book and call her back with cold dread filling up in my stomach.

"It's what you think sweetie. He's gone."

I cry and cry. I have to put the phone down so I can cry. I pick up the courage to stand up. I knock on Angie's door and walk in.

"He's dead Ange."

"Oh Annabella I'm sorry."

I cry onto her and she just hugs me. No words are said, what could we say? Everything has broken down;

my family are broken, in more ways than one. How do we carry on from this? How can we carry on normally with life?

I cry some more, telling Angie how much I hate this, how I hate what has happened to us. She speaks wisely about being strong and how he would be happy now. I don't hear exactly what she says, I feel too miserable to listen. I feel a sudden urge to be by myself, to mourn by myself. I never want people near me when I feel sad. I just feel awkward if someone does try to help me.

I tell her I need some time alone and then leave her room. I sit on the bed in my own borrowed room and just stare out of the window. Outside, the sun shines brilliantly on London. People are walking down the street, going about their normal routine. A tour bus sits opposite. Waiting to charge people a fortune to see the sights. I sit on the bed, with pain pouring through my heart. My life has been destroyed, but the world carries on.

21

I just need to lie here in bed.
I don't need to get up yet. Not yet.
I feel so . . . numb.
Grandma has gone.
Grandad has gone.
Dad is living somewhere else.
Mum is distraught.
I have quit university. I never quit anything. But I have quit this.
We have no money, and jobs are getting harder to come by.
My mind is dark. My soul is heavy.
I am ill. But not much can be done for the mind.
I feel like my life has broken. It has shattered into thousands of tiny pieces.
They just lie on the floor around me.
Dark and devastated.
I try to pick a piece up but I drop it. It has left a cut on my hand.
I am too scared to try again.

'Look at how pathetic you are Annabella.
Look at yourself.
The wannabe actress who will probably amount to nothing.
You can't even find the actor side of you, can you?
It has abandoned you.

Just like everything else.

Just like everybody else.

You can't even get a job. You let the depression take over.

You lost the people you loved.

You lost yourself.

You are pathetic Annabella. Stay in this hole you so desperately don't want to leave.

You are afraid. You are weak.

You can't even fight, because you are scared of losing more.

You are weak. YOU ARE WEAK!'

I AM NOT!

There is a glass piece of myself on the floor. I slowly bend down, and reach towards it. Maybe if I am careful, I won't scratch myself too badly.

I wrap my fingers around the piece of my life, and lift it from the ground. This piece of my life says, 'To write'.

I feel giddy with excitement and pick up another piece of my life. This one says, 'To travel'.

So that is what I must do. I must write and I must travel. I waste no time in telling my mum what I intend to do. She must see something different in my eyes because she nods her head and says okay.

So these are the only things I can hold on too, but I must work on what I have got. I cannot see anything else in my life. But maybe that is okay. I have something to start rebuilding my life with, and I intend carry on.

I can be changed by what happens to me. But I refuse to be reduced by it.—Maya Angelou

22

He choked to death. My mum had parked the car and ran to the door, but it was locked. It was the early hours of the morning; the only door open was on the other side of the hospital.

She ran as fast as she could. Through the doors, through the hospital corridors back to the other side, the ward grandad was on. He had been placed in a little room by himself. His eyes were still open. Mum thought he was still alive. He's dead, a nurse told her. The nurse left mum alone with him, she sat by his side and held his hand.

"Dad, I'm so sorry I wasn't here, I'm so sorry we never got along. Please forgive me."

I know he would be happy. Happy to no longer be living on this earth without the woman he loved. But now we are left to carry on.

We wait for a while to get his death certificate. People in the hospital aren't happy about his cause of death. I did think it was strange. He came into the ward thirteen days before his death. I had been there for the first eight days. He could walk and talk, escape and jump onto busses. He made his own drinks (never meals that was always my grans job, and then ours.) He was very fit, very active. Within eight days he could no longer walk, no longer stand, no longer sit up in a chair. He was not given medication, he was not given food. He was eventually nil by mouth. The bones in his cheeks, arms, chest and legs were visible, shockingly visible. It took my gran three months to get to that stage of bone showing through; for my grandad it took four days. He could not move. He was not fitted with a catheter. When he did need the toilet my mum would have to walk through the corridors, trying to find someone to help him. When someone did arrive, huffing and puffing at us, he was hoisted up screaming. I don't want to think that for the other times he was just left there to soil himself. I can't bear to imagine that neglect on him.

When we registered his death we were asked again if we were happy with the cause of death. We didn't know. He had choked even though he had not eaten in days. But he could have choked on his own body fluids. But is that worse? Should he have got into this state in the first place? We don't know. We are so numb with everything.

A social worker went to ask for his medical records. But for the first time in her entire career, she was refused them. For the first time in thirty years she was refused medical records. It may be okay to do so, but for us it just screams even louder that something strange is going on here.

Different doctors have told us to complain. They have told us to report what has gone on. Was my grandad neglected? Was his death avoidable? Was his suffering avoidable?

We tell ourselves that he is happy, he is with grandma now. But did he suffer? The question haunts us deeply. Blame and guilt set in, did we watch him suffer, and do nothing? Did we watch him die slowly, painfully, and let it all happen?

There are less people at grandad's funeral. I remember him telling me about his role in World War II. He was in the submarines, he had a name for what he did but I stupidly can't remember it. He would be part of the crew that would look for naval mines. He put down the heroics, making it seem like his job was cleaning pots. But going ahead to search out these explosive devises I would say was very brave indeed. He did some nursing at some point too; I was surprised to think of my grandad caring for people, being the nurse. But he did.

I feel bitter for him. I feel bitter for the thanks he received when the end came. There was an old veteran in the news recently, speaking about how he had to sell his war medals so he could pay for a care home. It's disgusting really, the thanks they receive. I am so bitter for them, so angry for them.

We have the same minister that we had for grandma. We like that we do, we like that he can give them both an equally important send off. We keep giggling throughout the service though because he keeps calling grandad Arthur, when his name was Albert. We really aren't offended, the minister is quite old and doesn't realise his mistake. He is so cute and cuddly we just want to give him a hug for his mistakes like you would want to do for a child.

He says good things about him though; he says good things about us. He tells us how he would be happy now, being with his wife. We agree he would be happy.

As the coffin is taken out of the chapel, Vera Lynn, 'We'll meet again' plays. It works well with him and grandma. He is back with her and finally happy.

He is lowered into the ground, there is a wooden board at the bottom and I think grandma is under that, the board is there so we don't have to see what has become of her. We throw the rose petals into the hole and we leave. That's it. They are both gone. Goodbye grandma and goodbye grandad. You are both together again.

23

The purpose of our lives is to be happy.
—Dalai Lama

I need to live. I need to be happy. I won't lie to you though. Sometimes it is nearly impossible for me to bring myself to think those words. Finding the strength to carry on is like finding air to breathe in water. But sometimes I can wake up, and not need to remind myself to get up. Sometimes I feel so alone. So in need for someone to tell me what to do, telling me it will be alright. I do not have that, but that doesn't mean I can't listen to myself.

I lie in bed and the sun hits my face. I cry; I'm not sure what I cry at, just routine I guess. I sit up and look towards the window. Please God give me strength to carry on.

'Give yourself the strength to carry on.'

When you hit an all-time low, and not literally hit by that song or the band, it's good to know that the only direction to move now is up. Losing yourself through dark times just means you have to find another window to show yourself again. Soon I hope to throw myself into

a new, lost wonderland, in the hope I find a familiar one.
Finding balance and happiness is part of finding yourself.
So maybe they could be the words of a desperate hippy.
But also the hope of a desperate soul.

24

"Yesterday you know what I had?"

"What?" my friends Rob and Meg ask me.

"Progress, a whole fifteen minutes of it."

I sat on the step in the garden to read my book and I saw some ants, and the ants were working really hard to move a huge fly. A blade of grass disrupted their progress and after a bit of time they realised that to carry on with what they were doing they needed to move the blade of grass. So they all worked in unison to move the grass and then got back to taking the fly away. I watched this transpire, these ants working to get to their goal.

Now the ant story has little relevance. But I'm getting into a lot of Buddhist teaching at the moment, and I realised that for fifteen minutes of watching these ants I had thought of nothing. My mind had been completely empty. I felt no anger for the people who hurt me. No anger for the hospitals. I didn't see the light leave my grandma's eyes as she took her last breath. I didn't imagine how my grandad choked to death. I didn't think about the pathetic existence I lead and how pathetic and sad I have become. I felt peaceful for the first time in years. I call that progress. Even if it was just for fifteen minutes.

25

I have to give Lucy away. We have been looking after her since grandad died. She hasn't been getting along with our dog Henri. She annoys him and it's been awful trying to separate them.

I can't do it reader. I can't bear to let her go. It is one of these situations where you know what you have to do. But you can't bear to go through with it.

She has slept in my room since we brought her home. She has cuddled up next to me in her little bed. I have put a cover over her when the heating broke and my room became an iceberg. Every strange noise she makes when she sleeps I rush across my bed and look over, making sure she is okay. I have become a bloody mother to what feels like a new born baby. Minus the crying and same species.

I laugh silently at her sleeping positions. She lies on her back with her legs sprawled apart like a terrible old tart. I will play games and pretend I am crying on the floor. She rushes to me and licks my face. Hoping to make me smile. She and Henri only get on when they decide to make a run for it.

The other day they got out of the house together and sprinted down the street. Ffyona ran after them as her friends walked up to see her. One of her friends saw the dogs running towards him and starting screaming and running away. He is afraid of dogs and decided that getting hit by a car would be less frightening then having to face a West Highland terrier. The other friends managed to coax Henri back to the house whilst Ffyona hoisted Lucy up from the ground. We think she was the main conspirator. It is always the little ones.

I laugh at these memories. I love these dogs so much. They are my babies. How can I let one be taken away?

A woman has come to the house. She knew gran, and grandma always said that she could have Lucy if anything were to happen to her. I hold Lucy for the last time. She looks at me with such beautiful brown eyes. How can I let her go?

I somehow hand her over to the woman. She gives Lucy a kiss and takes her away to her car. I stand there, staring as she puts my Lucy into the back seat. The woman waves goodbye and gets into her car. The ignition starts, she is driving away. I walk forward. No! I cannot let her go. I cannot lose another. The car is leaving, moving faster down the street. I run down the drive, gathering speed as I charge down the pavement. The woman turns on her indicator. She is about to leave. I try to shout but tears overcome me. I run faster than ever to reach her.

The car turns. No, please God let them stop. I get to the end but already they are half way down the road. I cannot reach them. I am too late.

I shrink to the floor. Weeping till I can't breathe. I have lost her. I will no longer look after her and watch her play. She will go to her new home. How can I know if she will be happy? How can I know she will be looked after?

Goodbye my little Lucy. I love you so much.

26

My body has just stopped itself now. There have been so many times in the past when I mentally could not bring myself to get out of bed. It seemed too difficult. Almost impossible to face the day, what more bad things could happen? Now it seems like that feeling has gone through my body, digging down through my muscles, taking root inside my bones. Keeping me locked in place, forcing me to lie here. Begging me to rest, to lie in sheets of safety. Hiding me from more danger. More hurt. No more pain, just rest.

I was asked to help a friend with her drama business as she and the children who attended were putting on a show. The idea of getting out seemed like a good idea at the time, but as the moment for me leaving arrived I felt such dread, such pathetic panic. I was scared. No, I was terrified. It was the first time in what felt like such a long time that I was going to get out, and act like a normal person again. I was going to meet people and surround myself with normal life. I felt my brain shut down, my thoughts cloud over. My body was shaking uncontrollably. All of a sudden I was on the floor crying. I told myself how much of a fool I was. Crying on the floor, scared to go out, acting like a child. When had I become so pathetic?

Mum got me to the car but I couldn't turn on the ignition. I just wept and wept. Mum told me I could just cancel but I didn't want to let a friend down. Not another friend anyway. She drove me to the school where the show was about to start. I sat there, frozen with fear. 'Act, pretend it's a film. It's not you anymore Annabella, be the actress you haven't been for so long.' I took a breath, and got out of the car. I somehow became the actress I had kept hidden.

27

Had the most amazing day today. I got up with the sun shining and the world so happy and busy. I chilled in my place for a bit then got ready and met the girls for lunch. After a great few hours of sushi and shopping, I got home and put on a fabulous outfit I had just bought. I was then picked up by a gorgeous guy I'm dating and we had an amazing dinner, followed of course by an amazing breakfast!

Okay so that's all a lie. I'm not one of the girls from Sex and the City and my life isn't that sweet. I am the nun from Manchester, the mental, emotional, fruit cake.

I'm trying not to complain, I'm trying not to be spoilt or selfish. I'm just a young person who should be starting her life. In fact, should have already started her life. I've fallen into this hole that that I can't yet climb from. I'm empty. I'm bitter. I'm lonely. What the hell happened to my life? An even better question, when will that life start?

28

Dear Grandma,

It is nearly the one year anniversary of when we found out you had cancer. I remember it so much Grandma. I remember how the doctors didn't even get a family member there with you when they told you.

I'm so happy you are with your family again. That you are happy and no longer in pain. But I am angry with how you were treated, and I am angry that they didn't give a damn. I'm angry that you are no longer here, because life has become empty.

I remember when I passed my driving test and you phoned me and asked for Annabella's taxi service and if they could bring a car round. I laughed and soon picked you up. You were so beautiful . . .

I wish I could phone you. Just talk to you. I want to see how your day is going and hear your laugh. I want to cry to you and hug you again. I want to see you smile. I want to watch 'The King's Speech' with you, because you didn't get to watch it. But most of all, I want you to know how much I love you. I love you so much grandma. I love you.

It hurts how much I miss you. I remember you taking your last breath. It was so horrible grandma. I wish I could have made you feel better. There is so much I could say, and I don't know how to say it all.

I just hope you are happy grandma. And I will try to be good. I hope I can make you proud someday. I love you grandma.

I love you.

Bella x

29

I thought I would watch the ceremonies of the Olympics online. They really were spectacular I must admit. It is lovely seeing our history re-created. A history we should be proud off. A history I am proud off. But I suddenly begin to feel quite disappointed. I would like to love my country so very much but there is some disappointment in it. A lot of people my age don't care about anyone or anything and then when I decide maybe we aren't so bad they decide to riot our cities for new jeans or phones.

Then we take money from our emergency services to pay for the mistakes of this recession. Take more money from people who don't have any more to give, meanwhile putting on a happy face and saying that we are British and we can get through anything. Yes we are British and we are brilliant but once we could say that with pride and respect. What happened?

I may seem unpatriotic but I can't help but notice how much we are falling. It just disappoints me seeing my home, the country I love and feel proud to be apart off, seems to be sinking so low.

30

At the time of writing this I see a lot of activity on Facebook about a girl who had committed suicide because she was bullied. There are groups and pages showing respect to her and people stating their hatred of bullying. She is not the only young person to have hurt herself because of bullying, but an example is being made from her death of how bullies ruin lives.

I see lots of people comment, giving her love and praise, and lots of others calling her a slag and an attention seeking bitch. Then the sympathetic group of people argue with the other group of people. In essence they bully each other. I begin to wonder if the sympathetic people are just giving false praise so they seem like the lovely heroic type. Or if the harsher people see through this and have some honesty in what they say. Are we all equally looking to be the hero, but enjoy playing the villain?

Is it bullies or is it just people in general? Are we all responsible in this? When we laugh at someone who acts or speaks or looks differently. Think a bad thought or say a bad word about somebody. Make them feel bad and not spare them a second thought or the consequences. Have we become such a sick, depraved species, that we feel happiness in the darkened whirlpool of another human beings pain? Are we just human or do we just not know enough about humanity?

When I was being bullied, I remember feeling scared. Scared that bullies would come to my home, or attack a family member instead. I once heard a story about bullies setting a girls hair on fire, when my bullies were stood behind me I moved my hair quickly over my shoulders, having a terrifying vision of them doing the same to me.

As the victim it is easy to feel isolated. Scared of everyone around you. Devastated that people could hate you so much. Believing that you are the excuse for why they do this. You are the only one to blame. Why do they pick on me and nobody else? I know so well how easy it is to believe this.

A teacher told me that one particular person was having problems at home. I remember screaming, "And how is that my fault!?" I have problems at home but do you see me bullying others? Do you see me hurting and hating and intimidating? It is not an excuse, so never think they have one. You never have an excuse to hurt someone else. A bully never has an excuse like that.

Another one I heard was, "They get bullied, and therefore they take their anger out on others." I repeat no! Because I was bullied, it did not mean I took my anger out on everyone around me. Two wrongs do not make a right. Why be bullied and then bully.

One girl said to the whole class that she hated me because I had big shoes and big hair. This I had to laugh at. She couldn't even remember my name. If I am hated because I have thick hair and not because I am an evil bitch I guess I'm not such a bad person after all.

I am not a victim, I am a survivor, and I thank God I can say that to myself.

31

"Grandma, do you want anything to eat?"
"No thank you."
"Not even a Bella snack?"
". . . Go on then."
I smile and run down to the kitchen. I get the cheese, ham and tomatoes and begin to slice them up. Lucy runs underneath my feet begging for food and I nearly double her weight in the cheese I give her.

Picking up the plate, I walk back up the stairs into grandma's room. She eats half the food and then puts it down. I begin to move it away from her but she grabs hold of my hand. I look at her beautiful hand holding so tightly onto mine. I wish I could spend the rest of my life frozen in this moment, holding my grandmas hand. Feeling the warmth through her skin. Her heart still beating.

I lie back on the bed next to her, still holding her hand. We lie there in silence, always silence now. Just making the most of that moment. The moments that we still have each other. She falls asleep again. This is when I can cry.

It's been a year since her death. A year since life shattered. When I held her hand I would tell myself, 'at least she is still here,' but I dreaded the day I would not be able to say that anymore.

I don't know how this year carried on. I don't know how we carried on. We just did. The months looking after grandad all felt the same. Suddenly when he wasn't there, we were faced with a void. To carry on with life. To carry on as if nothing had happened.

As it got to the one year mark however, it felt like a small shadow had lifted. I admit now, it is less sharp the pain. We can go through most of the day not thinking about one year ago. Although the nights are always there to haunt us with the memories, the nightmares. But I can wake in the morning. The sun's rays blazing through my window. I can almost feel happy.

I don't want to think of the people who hurt me in the past anymore. There are people responsible for my depression. But I don't want to blame or hate anymore. I have something with me, this blackness that has been my constant companion for four years. It may be there for the rest of my life. But it doesn't need to control me. Not anymore. I want to live my life, and I want to live a happy one. Because if I am honest, I think I deserve it. Or maybe I am just too stubborn to accept life will always be crap. I want to be happy, and I want my family to be happy. I want grandma and grandad to be proud of me. She was always so upset when I was having my bad days.

We go out for a meal, all together as a family. We take a detour home as there has been an accident on the motorway, and finally arrive. Dad pushes Ffyona across the hall and runs to the downstairs bathroom, Ffyona and Jonathan race upstairs to the other bathrooms.

It's been a good day; we were like a family again. Soon dad has to leave and we carry on with the rest of our night. I cry again when I go to bed, crying with such deep loneliness. I speak to grandma again and tell her I love her. I apologise to her again, telling her I'm sorry I didn't help her enough in those final minutes. I really miss her. I miss her so much the weight of it makes it difficult to breathe. One year ago, you were taken from me.

32

I look in the mirror and ask myself, 'what do you see?' I see lips stretched with bitterness. Cut from the times I had bitten down trying not to cry.

I see eyes full of sadness. Full of anger. Underneath is the hollow, darkened skin, courtesy of years of disturbed sleep. A face so aged, so much older than how it should look.

I am tired, and I am afraid. I am afraid of more pain. I am afraid for my family. I am afraid for myself.

I wished for something to dissolve the pain in my mind. Instead the darkness keeps my buried, teasing me with the beauty of the sun and the blue sky. It then swallows me back, burying me once more in my blackened hole.

Disappointment pours from the friends I should be able to trust, and the services that should not have let us down. In this world of disappointed hopes, how can the light seep through? How can happiness be felt? I look into the mirror and ask myself, 'what do you see?' I see a creature in pain, surrounded by darkness, crying in vain.

33

When I would feel sad and alone, I would just go out into the garden and look up at the stars. Suddenly I would feel such peace.

The sky would be a clear navy blue. With maybe only a few stray clouds. The stars would shine so bright. The brightest one I imagine is grandma. I smile up at the star, pretending she is smiling back.

But the moon, the moon lights up the night sky like a beacon. Her light so pure and beautiful. In the darkness of this world I can look up at her and feel safe again. I am no longer blinded by the darkness. I have that small shred of light. That tiny beacon of hope.

The night chill settles over me and I begin to shiver. I must, so reluctantly, leave my calm night sky, with all its beauty and freedom, and return to shelter, back into reality. Back to the harsh truth, and prepare for the start of a new day.

34

"What is life? It is the flash of a firefly in the night. It is the breath of a buffalo in the wintertime. It is the little shadow which runs across the grass and loses itself in the sunset."—Crowfoot.

Are you grieving for someone? Are you grieving for life? For yourself? It's okay. It's okay to cry. To scream. To hurt. It means you cared enough for something. Life is short. Too short.

Sometimes I can complain as I do about how crap things can be. But it takes just a moment to watch a sunset, to watch someone you love smile, to do something amazing. To feel something amazing. Take a breath and then another. Listen to the beat of your heart. Day after day, night after night, you realise you have done something so brave, you have carried on. You haven't given up. One day you will realise that for a moment. You forgot the pain. You forgot the hurt. You forgot the grief. I don't know when you will feel that. I just know that you will. In three days I turn twenty. Two decades of my life, only two decades. It isn't long.

Since life fell apart, I have only just found the courage to cry. Not cry from pain. I've done that for too long. I mean just cry for myself. Cry because I needed to. I

168

needed to remind myself that I am trying. I needed to remind myself that I am okay. I am okay.

I have lost important people. But I haven't lost them forever. I even lost a part of myself. I can't promise to always be this optimistic. I can't promise that my life will always be such a gift. I can just cry with the knowledge that I don't need to be so scared. I don't need to feel so lost. I'm crying and I am okay.

35

Just to sound like a soap opera to you, my dog, my beautiful Henri has cancer. Mum found a lump in his mouth, the next day we were at the vet. It was on my birthday. A piece of it was removed for testing, a few days later we found out it was a tumour. He has one on his tail too. The cancer has spread all through his body and it's going into his lungs. Soon he won't be able to eat, when this happens we will have to put him to sleep. He could choke at any time we have been told also. I would like to say that life won't always be shit. But I keep being proven otherwise. What the hell is happening to my family?

I don't think many people would really understand why I would be so devastated about a dog. But he has a personality, his own little traits. He doesn't like dog food he prefers caviar, the little snob. He can get grumpy with us. But he can also be very happy and want to cuddle and play.

I hand feed him now. He can eat normally but he has decided me being his butler is far more glamorous. He only likes me feeding him, which makes me feel special I must admit.

The knowing is hard though. One day he will be gone. His bed will be empty; his toys will have no owner. It will be so odd, so different. I don't want to lose him; I don't want to lose more. That constant fear of losing more haunts me. More pain, more hurt, more loss.

The day we got him, dad picked us up from school. Mum was waiting at the corner of our street. Holding a bundle in a little blue and white blanket. I thought mum had, had a baby! She slowly turned round the bundle and I saw a little black nose peeping out. I thought it was a strange looking baby. She turned him all the way round and a little golden retriever puppy was staring out from the blanket. He was so beautiful, me and Fe screamed, "a puppy, a puppy!" I was so happy.

In the kennel his brothers were in the same little room as him but he was the only one not jumping up at the window. He sat with his back towards the people looking, and would turn his head every so often to stare at viewers with disapproval. My dad knew that was the dog he was going to get mum. The dog with the almost human character.

36

I am lying down on the bed next to her again, it all feels so real. My grandma, my beautiful grandma is just looking at me smiling so beautifully. I smile back, so happy, so blissfully happy. Grandma is still with me.

Suddenly the scene around me begins to fade; the walls and carpets melt away. The bed begins to evaporate underneath me. Grandma disappears in front of me, it's all pretend, and it is all a dream. I begin to wake from my slumber, tears roll down my face. I wake up fully and begin to sob. I am in my bed, it is morning. It was all just a dream, such a life like dream. She's not here, wake up.

37

I thought I would be good and go on some kind of fitness regime. I decided soon I would be slim and gorgeous and totally sexy and that was the end of it. I registered with the gym near my house and thought I would shock everyone by actually going in.

I got on the exercise bike first thinking sitting down and moving my legs would be quite easy to do. I didn't really realised how long I was there for as I had noticed some hot guys walk in. There was myself and an old woman in the gym so I thought I may have stood a good chance. I spotted my friend Jane walking through the doors and decided that I would get of the bike and do a sexy walk towards her. I did not consider these next complications. First, I got off the wrong side of the bike. Not that there is a right side, but then I thought I could leave the bike area by walking between my bike and the bike beside me. Unfortunately I have boobs. These only got bigger recently by too much overindulgence of comfort food. As I walked sideways between the bike handles I got myself stuck between them. After lodging myself out with a type of sideways, bend down, penguin walk I managed to free myself from my fitness cage.

Then I misjudged the strength in my legs and how I probably wasn't ready yet to take my weight after the strenuous exercise. A step had somehow found itself in my path and I did not see it. I walked down suddenly facing too much of a drop than what I was originally prepared for. All of a sudden my leg gave way and I fell, toppling to the floor. In front of the hot guys. I ungracefully hurled myself up and had the nerve to attempt some prideful womanly walk away from the scene of the crime. Real Bridget Jones moment.

I thought my friend had not seen as she was looking at a notice board at the time. I stood beside her and looked with her.

"You just fell didn't you?"

"Yes." I thought it best to go home after that and maybe take a break from the gym for a while.

I decided to get my hair done by our lovely friend Angie, my drama teacher's sister. For so long I hadn't slept properly. So long I had cried till I could hardly see. Worn old clothes, the only ones easy enough to throw on when I needed to care for grandad. They say getting your hair done helps. It did. I felt pretty all of a sudden. Pretty and confident to walk out and face the world. A trip to the cinema sounds like a good idea.

Later that day I went to see Skyfall. Probably the best film I had seen in a long time. David Craig and Javier Bardem were just amazing. Dame Judi Dench was fantastic as usual! As the film focuses more on wonderful Britain I have decided that possibly the only few good things that make Britain wonderful as it once was, is probably our films and actors. Of course that is not all that makes Britain great but in my current circumstances I can't see much other brilliance.

Our relatives from Australia came to stay with us, Fiona and Athol. When I decided I wanted to travel, the first place I intended to go was Australia. I don't know why I picked the furthest and most expensive destination. Something just calls me there. Now our relatives are here I can't wait to hear what the place is really like! Athol likes to call me 'Pom' a lot. I still don't know why they call the English that.

I make some chocolate cake and ginger cake and our guests are quite impressed with my baking skills. I don't mention that the ingredients are from a packet. They tell me about the house they have and all the land that surround it. I am enchanted by their story. Even their warnings of crocodiles and dangerous insects do not deter me from my dreams of traveling down under. They show us pictures of their home and Athol shows me which of the rooms I can have. They have invited me to stay with them, and I feel like I could jump to heaven with the exhilaration I feel. I will visit them soon. The thought of it makes me shake with excitement.

38

"I'm dreaming of a White Christmas.'

I sit very happily watching the end of 'White Christmas'. The film is definitely one of my all-time favourites.

I have adopted the seat nearest to the Christmas tree. Here I can be closer to the very beautiful but very old decorations. One of the decorations is a little rocking horse with my name and the year 1992 painted on it. I have had this since I was a baby. My first Christmas. My sister has one just like it. There is a little angel there also which my mum remembers from when she was a child, but because I value my own life I won't tell you how old that is.

The tree reaches right up to the ceiling. We put the little yellow lights on first, followed by the ribbon and then the decorations. This tree really is the best one we have ever had. The best thing about it though is the smell, the smell of pine I absolutely adore.

After much persuading I had finally convinced mum to get a real tree again. We had stopped with the real tree because we bought a big fake one a few years before. Nothing could beat the real thing though.

Every year we would go to Newbank garden centre near our home. What makes this garden centre special is its sentimental value. We have been going here since we were children. In later years they added a little room which stored really old style cakes and biscuits. Shortbreads, ginger cakes, toffees and teddy bear cookies occupy the tables. Next to that is a room filled with old style juices and jars with peppers and chillies in them.

The best part is the Christmas room they added. It isn't always a Christmas room but when it gets near to the holiday season they fill the entire room with Christmas decorations and room ideas. Once we overdose with the splendour of this room, we finally charge outside to look for the perfect Christmas tree. Usually there is a big argument about whose tree is the best, and even though we know dad will pick the one mum has chosen we still hope ours will be the winner.

This year mum and I went by ourselves. We hadn't planned to get the tree it just happened. We found the biggest tree there; it had no bare parts, just full of lovely branches all the way down. It took a second for us to decide that was it, this is the one.

We gave it to the guy who wrapped it up and left it waited by the gate for us. When it was time to get it in the boot we hadn't really thought about the mechanics. For one it really was frigging huge! Secondly, we were meant to be picking Fe up from college soon. Thankfully it fit through the boot and up to the front seat, but we still had Ffyona to consider. She got a shock when she opened the door; luckily she managed to bend herself in somehow.

But this was it, this was the result, and it was so worth it. I sat staring up at the beautiful tree, feeling content and happy. I love Christmas. I admit it isn't as exciting as when I was a kid, but I feel more grateful at this time of year, which we really should feel.

I do think Christmas has been warped a little by people over the years. We just want presents and then want the food, once it's gone that's it. We all know it is a celebration of the birth of Jesus, but if you aren't very religious what else can it mean?

Charles Dickens was right when he wrote his book. I watch The Muppets version of 'A Christmas Carol'. I decided long ago that this was my favourite version, probably because it was the version we always watched when I was a child. It is the time to be thankful for what you have, to be grateful and happy with the good things in life. To help people less fortunate than yourself and be happy, well isn't that really the obvious thing to be at Christmas? Thankful, helpful, happy?

Christmas week, we watch films and play games. We try so hard to have a good time, and we somehow do. For a while I just want to forget everything. Forget the past year and just live in today. Some of Henri's presents are already under the tree. He knows they are his because he keeps sitting near them trying to rip them open. We have gone all out for him this year, the knowledge that this will be his last Christmas hangs over us like a dark cloud. We try to keep happy though, we keep happy for him.

On Christmas day I am beyond happy with my gifts. I got a long, silk night dress I have been wanting for ages. At least it seems long, until I add my boobs, hips and arse and then it drastically gets shorter. I got the Poirot box set (I love Poirot), books and I'm not the least bit sorry to say I also got a Woody doll from Toy Story. I'm not even ashamed about that, I wanted him the most!

I love to watch my family's faces as they open their presents. Henri is probably the most excited and begins to play with his new toys. Dad isn't usually here on

Christmas Day; it's really busy for cinemas on Christmas. Partly because there are others who don't celebrate the holiday and partly because once the presents are opened, some people get bored and decide to go off and watch a film. We have a second Christmas on Boxing Day, which is also Jon's birthday, so it works out brilliantly.

New Year is never exciting; we watch the celebrations on the television. 2012 has been the year for the British but I don't feel like joining in with the celebrations. We have nothing to celebrate. It has been shit, so disgustingly shit. We keep some hope though, somewhere we find hope. We say maybe 2013 will be better. Maybe it can only get better from here.

My mum kisses me goodnight and I am left alone in the living room, watching the fireworks on the screen light up London. I do hope for a better year. I hope so desperately that life gets better for my family. I wish for nothing more than for them to be happy. I imagine that somewhere there is a shooting star, soaring through the sky, granting my wish. That's how it works in the movies. I could just be a child again and pretend my dreams will come true.

I turn everything off and go up to my room. I hope for all the people who need hope, I hope for mummy, daddy, my sister, my brother, and Henri of course. I hope for myself.

Happy New Year.

39

Dear Grandma,

I am writing a book! I started writing when everything bad was going on. I wrote and wrote for what felt like forever. I needed to tell people what was going on. How you had been treated, how hard things had got.

I never thought you would die. I hoped I would be able to think of just the good times. But there was so much bad at the end. I don't want to just think about the end though. I want to think about the good times too. Because there was so many good times grandma. I remember whenever mum got something you had to get it too. You would walk in with brand new shoes and show them off. We would complement you and tell you how glamorous you looked and you would be very happy with that.

Sometimes I want to pick up the phone to ask you if you want to go out somewhere, then I remember you are far away. If I am out I see people everywhere, laughing and having fun. I wish so desperately that could be us again. Every store, every cafe, still house the shadows of where you walked, where you sat.

I had to write about us, but I want people to know that it wasn't always so bad. I had most of my life to laugh and live, to be completely happy knowing you were there.

Our story is going to be a book. I hope you don't mind that. I hope I make you proud.

I want to be happy again grandma. I want us all to be happy. I think we will be, of course life will never be the same. If I didn't try to be happy, I think that would be an insult to you. You would encourage me to live, go out clubbing, get a boyfriend. You were always so worried I would be alone. Please don't worry anymore. I doubt I will be the clubbing person, and Johnny Depp is taken but I will try to live grandma. I promise I will make you proud. I will keep you up to date with things gran. Watch over mum, she needs you more than ever. I love you grandma, don't be drinking too much whiskey up there.

Bella x

40

"I start to feel like I can't maintain the façade any longer that I may just start to show through. And I wish I knew what was wrong. Maybe something about how stupid my whole life is. I don't know. Why does the rest of the world put up with the hypocrisy, the need to put a happy face on sorrow, the need to keep on keeping on? I don't know the answer; I know only that I can't. I don't want any more vicissitudes, I don't want any more of this try, try again stuff. I just don't want out. I've had it. I am so tired. I am twenty and I am already exhausted."—Elizabeth Wurtzel.

This quote always seemed so true to me. It made such sense, sense for what I was feeling, am feeling. I feel like a walking hypocrite. I can feel so tired of life. So sad, sadness dripping off my bones, my muscles, my soul. Yet sometimes there would be this other part of me. This other part that would turn up out of nowhere and shout at me. Telling me to stop being so god damn stupid. It would tell me to get up and face the world, life was too short to wallow in darkness. Too precious to let myself sink into my drowning pit of despair.

One day depression entered my life, I can't change that. I suddenly found myself in a dark room, with all the windows bordered up. Some days I would feel okay, and the boards would be removed. Other days I felt strong enough to pull them off myself. It was so exhilarating to see the sun again. The beautiful light taking out the darkness. Banishing out my cold and dreary surroundings. I know I can't always control this room. That is depression. But that doesn't mean I won't try.

I don't know what or who this other part of myself is. The part that makes me want to fight and love and live. Maybe it is the true part of us all. The part that knows that no matter how many tunnels of shit you crawl through, eventually the tunnel will stop. You will crawl out, dirty and tired, and see the sun shining again. Breathe the fresh air, and take a well-deserved bath.

I hope for happiness. I hope for life. I am happy, because I didn't give up. Sometimes I wake up and the sun shines his light. My room is no longer in darkness.

41

"Angie, have you ever gone to bed fully clothed, and woken up the next morning, somehow completely, erm, naked?"

"No!" She responded shocked.

"Oh yeah, me neither."

"What did you do?"

"It wasn't my fault! I went to bed in my nightwear, and this morning I realised I was slightly cold, and slightly . . . naked."

"How the hell did you get naked during the night?"

"Well I don't know that's why I was asking you!"

"You might have slept walk, kind of thing."

"Oh I'm totally not insane, just casually shout out in my sleep and now I like to flash in my sleep too!"

"Well we knew you were insane anyway."

"Thanks Ange, I'm really feeling your love for me there."

"You're welcome Bella."

"I was incredibly disappointed not to see a man next to me, which would have made my day incredibly more exciting."

"I think it would us all."

"I hadn't even been drinking either."

"Definitely just insane then." Angie and I sat sipping our drinks for a while. Angie is use to me and my strange ways of thinking, so I could bring up conversations that included nudity or other such subjects.

"Are you coming to my meal?" She asked.

"Wouldn't miss it, may have to sell myself to pay for it though."

"Okay, just don't catch anything." She takes a sip of her drink as I stare out the window.

"You know it took me eighteen years to realise T.G.I. Friday's meant, Thank God it's Friday."

"Seriously?" She looked practically appalled at me.

"Yeah, and KFC was Kentucky fried chicken. I only realised that one a few weeks ago."

"You are so blonde."

"Hey! No one goes round saying they want some Kentucky fried chicken do they? They say KFC, how do you know unless you aren't told these things!"

"Use your brain and work it out."

"It's not always that simple Ange." She started laughing at me. It is escapes like this you need I guess. Talking about complete crap, because why the hell not!

"You want a lift to work?" I asked her.

"Oh yes please!" Vanilla Ice began playing on the radio; we couldn't help curving our heads from side to side as 'Ice Ice Baby' boomed through the speakers. The cheesy songs are always the best.

"Have a good day." I shouted through the open window.

"I will! Thanks for the lift! Text me if you want to talk."

"Will do, bye!" There are always some people who do care.

42

It is March, and it is snowing. I stand outside with Henri as he has a wander through the snowy carpet. It is freezing but I don't care. I stand outside watching him play, my thoughts turn morbid as I wonder if this will be the last snowfall he will experience.

I have just finished writing to my wonderful friend Hannah, telling her that there may not be any good news to tell her for a while yet. Henri will get worse. The complaint letters to the hospitals have gone through and I fear the result. There is no end yet. We are in a tunnel, it is pitch black. I imagine a light, somewhere in the darkness. But I could be dreaming, hoping too much. I am hoping it is the end of this long and god forsaken tunnel. I know there will be the end to the darkness. I know we will come out of it eventually. I just don't know when. We keep saying how things will get better. I just wish better was today.

I enjoy the snow. We are a nation; very good at complaining about how there is no snow for Christmas. Then when it does arrive we complain about how much we hate it. We forget when we were children, seeing snow for what felt like the first time, being completely spellbound by its presence. All the snowballs we fought with and snowmen we brought to life. The hills we sledged down. The more romantic of us wanting the perfect kiss in it. Just seeing the first snowflake, fall from the sky, watching it land softly on your skin. The smile when you saw it, the smile on children's faces when they see it.

I apologise for my random turn of thoughts, but I must find pleasure in the simplest of things. But is there anything wrong in finding happiness in the simpler things? Finding peace in the simple pleasures life gives us?

43

Sometimes I think I'm going mad. I stand in my room wild eyed. Wanting to say things I can't understand, needing to scream things I cannot say. I hold a teddy, some childlike need for a friend, wanting it to listen as I speak my thoughts. Pretending it's the friend I need desperately. A friend who won't disappoint. Who listens without judgement. Who understands and cares.

My breathing quickens. So fast I can't catch it. I cry in panic, with sadness and loneliness. Crying with such deep, heart-breaking loneliness. I am weak again. I am weak from life. People say you are given your life because you are strong enough to live it. I don't think I am strong enough. I don't think I am strong enough at all.

I have so many hopes, and I fear each one. I fear them never happening. I fear this continuous dark pit of despair that keep me hostage. I want to see the sunshine so badly I ache with the longing.

A full moon shines through my window. Such pure brilliant white light shines back at me through the darkened sky. I raise my tear streaked face to it and slowly breathe. Breathe. Breathe.

44

The voice recorder opens its secrets with a slow buzz. There is waiting, waiting for her voice to begin her narrative.

"She explained to us what would happen, that he would feel no pain. I was going to stay with him but then dad turned up, I was glad about that because I knew Henri would be happy to see him.

Dad didn't want me seeing that again because I had seen gran go, so he told me to sit outside.

Eventually I was put in a room on my own and the door was left open.

An RSPCA woman came in and after a while she brought out a dog. She and the dog were in the next room and the dog kept weeing everywhere."

She laughs.

"The dog was really skinny, could see the bones, it had a big cut round his neck where a collar would have been, like it was too tight and cut into him . . . And he was being taken to a dog's home.

Then she mentioned about a postmortem on another dog and her puppy and she said the mum and the puppy had been starved to death . . . And I was so angry because the dogs here had been abused and Henri was being put to sleep in the room behind me, and Henri was so loved. He was so loved.

After a few people came in to ask if I was okay, Michelle the vet came in and she said that he'd gone."

She begins to sob.

"She said it was very peaceful like he had just gone to sleep. I asked if I could see him because I had just seen this abused dog and I felt I had to see Henri because he wasn't, he wasn't abused he was loved.

So, she took me through the back and just explained what happened and I walked in and she said take as long as you want."

She cries even more.

"He was on the floor mum was sat in front and dad near his head and I went round to his back, my hand instantly went to his stomach. I was being silly expecting my hand to rise up because it would move when he breathed. And it hit me, there was no movement, there was no breathing.

For ages he had been making a weird breathing sound because he was struggling with the cancer in his head. But this time there was silence.

Mum was crying and dad's eyes were red, I could tell he had been crying.

Henri's eyes, they were open a little bit

And he was lay . . . he was lay down it looked like he was just sleeping.

I felt his tummy and I stroked him and I kept stroking him, and I went to his head and I kissed him and I kept kissing. Then I felt round him one more time, and I told him he would be happy, he would no longer be in pain anymore. He would be with grandma, and she would be giving him loads of biscuits like she once did. He would be eating lots of food and he would be okay because he would be happy and he would be with gran."

Her story became more and more difficult to hear as her crying took over.

"I told him I loved him and we kissed him again and then we left. It was yesterday when this happened . . . It hurts so much. We love him so much. I don't know what to say. Everything is so awful.

Everywhere I went in the house, he should have been in the lounge, he should have been in the kitchen and he should have been playing in the garden.

There were still the stains of blood where he had lay and I didn't want to wash them away. I didn't want to wash them away."

She audibly breaks down. After some silence she continues.

"I can't wait to move now. It's just this house; I can't imagine not having him because he was a part of our lives. Now we go through the house and he's not following us. I can't hear his claws on the kitchen floor. He's not walking about, I can't hear him panting and I can't hear him drinking.

He should be here and he's not.

I want to feed him anything he wants. I want to play our game of hide and seek. I would hide and he would find me and he would run around to look for me and when he did he would give me a look like he wanted to tell me off for hiding . . . he would always look for me."

More silence.

"Lost everyone . . ."

"Last night I didn't want to think about it, it hurt too much so I just had to imagine like I was in a film and doing my drama and it stopped the pain.

What the hell has happened to us?"

45

The conditions I mentioned earlier for what my brother has include Autism, Asperger's. Autism is a disorder which mostly causes difficulties with social interaction. He can get worried and anxious when put in difficult situations especially surrounded by people. We have to tell him what he needs to do sometimes so he can look after himself. Other than that he lives a very normal life. He loves to go walking and take pictures. He takes the most fantastic photos we are always spellbound when he shows them to us.

We can have conversations about anything and everything. He can get confused with emotions, handling and showing his own feelings. But if he is upset he will show us he is upset. If we are upset he will be the first one to hold us and tell us things will be okay. He has brilliant social workers who have helped him understand his condition better, Bev and Gillian. We are lucky to have these women helping him and us to understand. Due to the recession however, cuts are also being made in regard to council workers.

The day we went to the Lake District, Jon had become very distant. The days after he got worse. He would stay in his room and not speak to anyone. We would ask what was wrong and would get a stuttering response. It was like he was scared to talk to us. After days and days of trying desperately to get an answer from him I managed to get some form of explanation. He had been working in a department store. Two men from this store had attacked him numerous times. They threatened him and walked him to a cash machine, several times, so that he could withdraw money and give it to them. He was so scared he couldn't tell us. The men had threatened to hurt Fe and myself if he did tell anyone. This is when his depression started.

The past couple of days Jon has been acting the same way he had all those years ago. Jon had seen one of the men in a pizza shop near our house. Hence him going downhill again. He hasn't slept for two days and neither have we. He has spent the past two nights walking into mine and my mum's room, talking to us about things that happened years and years ago.

He spoke about things that happened as a child. How they still upset him. How he could not move on from these issues that had taken place. Things like, not getting a good grade in the math test. One incident where a girl wasn't very nice to him. He did not speak about the more 'serious' issues that had happened. Grandma's death and the effect it had on him, or the bastards that had hurt him so much. He could only talk about the silly, little problems. Of course any problem, no matter how big or small needs resolving.

Now, I would be the biggest hypocrite in the world if I told people to, 'Move on, get over it.' I would never say that because I know how difficult it is too move on sometimes. Bloody hell, it took something like my gran's death for me to finally let go off the things that happened to me in school. I can't promise forgiveness. I can't promise to forget. Sometimes bad things happen, and many times, the bad things are done by the people around us.

The people that hurt me do not feel pain on my behalf. They don't feel sadness or regret. The people that hurt my brother do not feel guilty for what they did. As far as any emotion goes to what they did, there are none. But why must there be on our part? Hate takes up the same energy that love does, and I don't want to waste my energy. I don't want to waste anymore of my life, on people that wouldn't waste their life on me. Moving on isn't that simple. But making the choice to try is. You can decide to be happy. Or you can decide not to be. I want to be happy. I want my family to be happy, and I'm bloody too stubborn not to try.

46

Well reader, after weeks of knowing nothing, weeks of wondering when we would finally leave and move on with our lives, we were finally told when we had to move. We drove as a family to Oldham. We signed our names on the dotted line. We were agreeing to leave our lives behind. For three days we were numb. For the four days afterward we were manic. We had a short time to pack up our lives. The three days we had wasted could have really come in handy for rounding up thirty years of, well shit. I have old certificates, photo albums, and toys. Everything packed away. Twelve boxes later I had packed all my books. Yes reader twelve boxes!

The past year we had also rented out grandma's house. The disgusting couple renting the house had completely trashed the place. They had also stopped paying the rent. When they moved out, the girl came back and stayed the night with another guy who was not her boyfriend. Nice, considering she recently just had a baby also. We have put this house up for sale. It was time to move on.

The packing had become very tedious and I could not sit on my floor for much longer. I decided to have a little walk to my usual haunts, for just one last time.

The cricket club I had so often sat at and where I had gone to parties looked suddenly strange and unfriendly. The country road to grandmas was no longer sunny and inviting. The horses that so often greeted me were no longer in sight. My high school, absent of students and teachers for the summer holidays seemed foreign to me. The houses, the streets, the parks, I no longer belonged too. They are no longer mine.

I must leave the ghost ship that was my home. I must wrap away the memories and leave them for someone else to open.

I journeyed back through my house and into my garden. No, no longer my house, no longer my garden. Goodbye to this chapter. Goodbye Bury, Goodbye Manchester. Goodbye to the good times and goodbye to the bad. If we can say goodbye to something that meant so much to us, maybe we can finally move on.

I walked into my bedroom, closed the door and let the world lull me into the comfortable darkness that comes with sleep. For the last time, I will fall asleep in this house.

The vans are packed. We are on our way. It was a difficult day loading thirty years of crap into the vans but we actually managed it. I said goodbye to my dear friends. To my butcher friend I would always chat with. To our good friends, Philomena and Tom and Pat from across the road. To our home.

After an hour of driving we finally reach our new home. Well our new home for about a year. We are staying in a beautiful, big farm house near Chester, just on the Welsh border. Our neighbours are currently a field of cows. This I absolutely love! I take a walk inside the house. There are wooden beams on the ceilings and old stone make up the walls. A large iron key, only seen in period drama shows on TV, opens the huge, solid front door.

Everything here is perfect! Well, perfect for me. I am blessed to finally feel such peace. I hope for a short time at least, we have no more worries. I hope for a longer time we have some happiness. I hope things start to happen in my life. I hope in a few months, once I turn twenty one, my life can finally begin again. I hope with all the life I have in my heart. Without hope, we have nothing.

47

"Annabella, some post for you outside, some package or something." My dad mysteriously said to me. Some package? What the bloody hell had I been ordering? Just before this, my sister and our friend Al had lead me outside under false pretences. They told me I needed to look at some cows in the field. It was a ruse to get me away from the front of the house but I fell for it. Strangely I did not question why they would want me to look at the cows. I was quite interested and even had a conversation about them. Yes I am that random.

After dad had told me to go outside for my post, I walked across the hallway and to the door. I had not realised everyone else was following close behind. My hand grasped the door handle and slowly pulled. There was a car in front of me. A beautiful, blue mini cooper convertible. I was in a state of shock, my eyes moved down to the bonnet where a long silver Happy 21st sign lay. Balloons had been placed round the wing mirrors.

Denial struck, believing nothing this beautiful could belong to me, but the realisation finally hit. This was mine. My own new car! I burst into tears, crying with complete and utter happiness. My mum and dad were crying with me just watching my face. I can't tell you how happy I was, am. Back at home, I had lost the thrill of driving. I had no confidence, no drive- literally. I had lost the enjoyment of it all. Driving from grans-shop-pharmacy-home. Most of the time when I was driving I was either crying to myself or being used shamelessly by my friends for lifts. Now I was away from all that and I had the most god damn sexy car to enjoy to myself.

A childhood notion for me also, was that a convertible was a luxury. That I would never own one in my life. I have suddenly become a very lucky and spoilt girl, reader. For a short time, I am going to say that rather proudly. I am lucky and I am happy.

48

Some mysterious entity stirs me from my slumber. I wake up dazed and confused. Wondering why I have woken up at such an ungodly hour.

The sunrise was bathing my room with a soft orange glow. I look between the gap in the curtains; my sleepy eyes could just about glimpse mist, floating along the ground.

The entrancing picture made my heart flutter. I shifted the covers of me and walked towards the window. The view welcoming me, took my breath away. The sun was shining through the big apple tree in the garden, casting vibrant rays on to certain areas of the ground.

The sky was a mixture of red, orange, pink and blue, painting the heavens with glorious artwork. I opened the window and inhaled the air. It was fresh, alive. Cleansed from the cold that had settled through the night. The cold now disappearing through the warmth of the sun.

Across the fields the mist was gliding through the grass, immersing the ground with a magnificent, white carpet. I could almost see Mr Darcy walking through the mist as he did in the film. I hoped anyway.

We decided to take a trip into Chester. I have completely fallen in love with this city. Some of the buildings here date back to maybe four hundred years ago, possibly longer! We walk through the centre, past the Grosvenor hotel. I look into shop windows; one in particular is selling a full size armour suit. Like the armoured statues you find in castles. We walk through the city, walking on top of the old city walls, bringing us closer to the river.

Little boats float along one side of the river, held in place only by small strips of rope. Old style huts shelter the people selling ice-cream from the hot sun. On the other side of the wall, tall Edwardian houses look down towards the river. I look into the windows and see flowers and small wooden boats occupying the window sills. Mum, dad, Fe and Jon are somewhere in front looking at an old plaque on the wall. We are like a family again. The sun is shining so bright, one of the last beautiful days of summer. I feel so happy. So happy and relaxed, for what feels like the first time in years.

I look into the other windows and spot a face staring out of one of them. It is an old man looking out at the scene below him. He must sense my gaze and turns towards me. He looks at me and smiles sadly. I smile back, wondering what could have caused his sorrow. There is something in his gaze I recognise. It's like desolation. Heartbreak. I feel alarmed because I know this look so well. His eyes bear the same resemblance to mine. To my family. It's a strain that somehow makes you different from others around you. It turns you into a ghost, not belonging in the spirit world but not really belonging to the living either. You are trapped, wandering between realms. Not being able to find where you truly belong. I look at this old man, and I am greeted by a fellow broken soul.

I turn my gaze away from him, to where I see my family waiting for me. I leave him staring sadly out of the window, watching the world carry on without him. I walk away in the beautiful sunshine.

49

My fingers grow numb from typing. I have told you my entire life. What has happened in my short life reader? Sometimes I wonder if I just dreamt it all. I could still be the girl with the long blonde hair. Smiling and laughing. I had dreams. I have dreams. I knew happiness. I know happiness. I lived. I loved. I lost. Why did these things need to happen? What could I possibly have learnt from them?

I have shown you what a life is like. How completely, beautiful and awful and strange it can be. Once upon a time, a path was made for me, and the bravest thing I can do, is walk it.

We all have our own paths to tread. I do not know why we must tumble. I do not know why we must fall. I cannot tell you why the sun or the rain wanders into our lives. Why the shadows of darkness can hide us from the light. Or why the light shines till we can no longer see.

I think I must go now. I must take a trip, and see what answers can come my way. I smile with sudden excitement. Tomorrow I leave.

50

So I may not travel the world yet. I will just go to the places of my home, and try to find myself again. I can't recognise who I see in the mirror. But I know the girl I once was, must be in there somewhere. I don't think I will get her back completely. But maybe in the destruction of ourselves, we can re-create an even better version.

I pack my little suitcase with a couple pairs of pants, tops and underwear, just quickly adding my writing gear and a few books on the back seat of my car.

"Are you sure you will be okay?"

"I will be fine mum, I promise. I will call you as soon as I get there." Mum looks at me with sudden loss. I didn't realise how hard this would be. I run to her and she takes me in her arms. We hug so fiercely, not wanting to let go of one another.

"I love you so much."

"I love you too mummy." I eventually let go of mum and walk to my sister.

"You be good missis, and look after everyone."

"I'm always good! You know I will." I hold her against me. A tear escapes down my cheek.

"I love you." She simply says to me.

"I love you more."

"I love you most!"

"Damn!" She laughs at having won the love you contest. Jon stands near, unsure of what to do. He is so brave, so beautifully brave.

"I love you Dangy." Dangy is what I use to call him when I was a child.

"I love you Annemeister." I smile up at him and give him a little fake punch in the arm. He laughs in reply.

I walk slowly to my car, and get in. My family are huddled together staring at me. I will be with you again soon. I promise.

I am leaving Chester. Driving further away from the place that had given my family much needed refuge. I keep driving, following the signs that simply said, 'The North.'

I had soon reached Gretna Green. I quickly stopped in the services, the services we always stop in for a bathroom break and a little rest. I pause to look at the old pictures hanging on the walls. Old photographs showing couples who had eloped years ago, desperate to be together.

I drive and drive, eventually reaching the road that holds a perfect view of the William Wallace monument. Eventually I reach Inverness, only an hour and a half to go till I get to Aultbea.

Every detail stays the same here, I hope this never changes. The sun's rays stream through the clouds, highlighting certain parts of the land. It's so big you can see where they point too. Over mountains I go, round streams and lochs. Goats and sheep stare as I drive by. The land is alive here. Everything is so wild and free. So fiercely beautiful.

I finally reach Aultbea. I turn right and drive round the beach, down the long stretch of road, bringing me nearer to our beautiful home. I park on the drive, turn off the ignition and get out. The pebbled driveway, tells of my arrival. Before I get my things I just decide to go into the house first. Opening the door I walk into the kitchen, everything is silent. I go through into the living room and stare out of the window. Looking out onto the beautiful views of the mountains and farmland.

I am completely alone. The realisation dawns on me gradually. I am not afraid through. I am in the only place I can escape from the world, from the hurt. I can't even escape that in my sleep most of the time.

I go back out and get my things, putting them in the bedroom. It will be getting dark soon, so maybe the first thing I should attempt is a fire. I build it up with logs and coal, putting in paper and firelighters here and there. I won't lie, it isn't brilliant, but at least I won't freeze. The smoke and the heat begin to cover my body, as the flames light up the gathering darkness in the room. Every so often the fire spits a little piece of burnt wood at me, making a little 'pop' sound echo through the air.

I think of how simple this is, how simple things use to be, back to a time when everything seemed like 'Hakuna Matata.' Life isn't life without hurt or pain or loss. Everything is a worry, everything is a challenge. But sometimes it's good to just escape to simplicity. Just to take a breather and try again. You can escape to the sweet pleasure of a simple nothing. Even if you just close your eyes and breathe in and out.

I rise late the following morning after a much needed rest. It is a beautiful day. I go to the front door and have a little fight with it to open; it stiffly complies and allows me to exit.

As I walk outside the sun blinds me like headlights on a foggy night. The sounds of sheep and the waves crashing against the rocks greet me. The wind blows fiercely, causing my hair to pick up high around me.

I look upon my beloved home, the mountains still looking as large and as fierce as ever. The farm houses are dotted around, showing other signs of life in this rural land.

I walk forward, my feet bare. The grass is harder here, much tougher. It probably needs to be to hold its own against the salty spray of the sea, carried in the ferocious winds.

Such peace settles over me. More peace than I have felt in years. I take one last look before walking back inside. Peace.

With no one else to talk to I talk to the sheep, just to keep my voice working. I write in my notebook and tell an unlucky sheep how good it is to write. The sheep looks at me with a mixture of boredom and contempt before strolling away to feast on more grass.

I shrug my shoulders at it and begin to write again. I pause for a second and look out to the island across the loch. If grandma could be anywhere, she would be here, in her old home. Maybe she is here with me now, maybe.

"Grandma . . . grandma . . . that sheep was awfully rude to me. I guess it can be though; I am just talking to a sheep. Are you happy gran? Being home with your family again? I think you will be because, well because you are here. You are home . . . I needed to be here grandma. I needed to come back. I have to start again. Rebuild myself. I need to put the full stop at the end of a chapter and start a new one. Maybe you can help me?"

I'm talking to the air but it feels quite normal. The sun has broken through the clouds, everything has become alive again. I put down my pen and pad and smile. I feel like a drive.

I drive down roads, through forests, round lakes, always in the mountains. Suddenly everything I write and think and feel envelopes me. The whole story, our story hits an ending. Everything begins to stumble together.

I park on a little passing place next to the road; I am at a particularly beautiful spot, with breath-taking scenery all around me. We always drive by here, but never stop to just look.

I climb over the fence and walk forward. The sun's rays touch down setting hundreds of diamonds free on to the ocean's surface. The mountains reign over the land, climbing so high they don't seem to end. I sit down on the grass and stare out onto this beautiful freedom and life stirs up in my mind.

I could forget the past, and forget the pain. Be happy and ignorant. Just forget. But if I forgot the past, I would be forgetting the people I love. I would be ignoring who they were and how much I miss them. I would be pretending the people I love with all my heart never left, because they never existed. Could I really let them go and be forgotten?

Maybe the pain of loss is the only thing you have left when the ones you love have gone. It means you once were not alone. Once the people you loved and cared about, once loved and cared about you too.

Because I knew a woman I loved with all my heart. Who raised me and cared for me. Who loved me more than life. I knew a man who cherished me the moment he first saw me. Who taught me how to swim and tie a tie. Who cried when I said I am going to travel and tried so hard to remember us when dementia said otherwise. I am lucky I had these beautiful people. I am lucky I was loved so much, and the pain I feel is all that is left of the love I felt back. Pain and love can blend so easily. It means we lived for something or someone.

Scars and fear are not to be ashamed off. It means we were hurt and broken, we found an upside down way of healing again. We admit to our flaws and even in the face of danger, we can show our courage.

We can cry and weep, give up completely. But somehow we take a step and then another. With time as our companion, we walk through the battlefield. Past the loss and pain. We climb steeply, stumble a few times and eventually reach the safe harbour. We can look back at the devastation, our devastation. Find pride in what we overcame. Relief in getting through it. Joy in ourselves.

The battlefield has and will always be there. But the strength you have, the strength I have, will help us. And if you are going through this now I say good luck, you will need it. But you aren't on your own. Keep stepping, keep fighting, and reach that mountain. Look back at your own battlefield. Look back, see it, feel it. Then walk on. I will and must keep doing this. I pray to God to lend me strength. Or maybe I just need to pray to myself. Life is hard, but I intend to live it. I just hope I can take big enough steps.

As I think this a sudden snap fills the air, disturbing my thoughts. I turn away from my view and slowly look around to discover the source of the noise. A stag stands near. Not so close I can see him perfectly, but close enough for me to be completely shell shocked at his presence. His coat looks bristly, I can see the muscle and power underneath. He stares patiently with eyes so dark and full. Several branches lunge out of his antlers; they seem to be pointing in every direction. He is so magnificent! I quickly remind myself to breathe and keep as calm as possible.

His head turns to look back at the mountains, the mountains I had just been gazing at. He looks calm, looking at the scenery he must be so use to by now. I can't help but to look with him.

I feel my grandma sat beside me, holding my hand again. Looking upon my view, silently telling me I am not alone. Grandad stands further behind at the car, looking at us both. Henri barks from within, happy and healthy again. None of them are in pain anymore.

Tears roll down my face as my heart pounds with love. I cannot see them, but I do not need to. They are here with me, within me. I can finally pick up my broken life and start again. I am strong enough. I am determined enough. I am enough.

I sit here alone, for a while longer, until my stag decides to leave me. An eagle flies somewhere overhead and I remember something I heard once. An eagle will fly above the storm and that is how she misses them. We are not eagles, we cannot fly above destruction. But if a rose can bloom in the snow, be trodden on and ripped apart. Grow from the ashes of burning debris, and still find the strength to carry on, and be more beautiful than before, surely we can too.

I will live in my pain. I will live in their love. I will live. And one day I will see them again.

Epilogue

I wasn't sure how I would end this book, and if I should start a new one. It seems I will write no matter what so we shall wait and see. I always said I will travel. At the time I was not able to jet off to somewhere exotic. Not many of us can when things are bad. But whether your dream is to travel, to find love, or just to be happy, you must make sure you chase it, that you chase it to the end of the world.

Right now I am on a plane, flying to some mysterious, strange land. I won't tell you the destination yet, because it is not the destination that matters, it is the journey. I am excited my dear reader, I can't wait for my life to begin again.

Fight through pain. Fight for happiness.

About the Author

Siobhan Mackenzie, 21, was born in Bury, Manchester, United Kingdom. She is one of three children. She has studied drama and dance for 10 years. She has written a collection of poems which have since been published in several books. Siobhan found the inspiration to write this book when similar incidents happened to herself and close friends and family. She currently resides in Cheshire.

Lightning Source UK Ltd.
Milton Keynes UK
UKOW05f1526191113

221419UK00001B/5/P